Christopher Levenson

Selected Poems 1964–1983

DOUGLAS DUNN

*Selected Poems
1964-1983*

faber and faber
LONDON · BOSTON

This selection first published in 1986
by Faber and Faber Limited
3 Queen Square London WC1N 3AU
Photoset by Wilmaset Birkenhead Wirral
Printed in Great Britain by
Redwood Burn Ltd Trowbridge Wiltshire
All rights reserved

Europa's Lover was first published
by Bloodaxe Books in 1982

British Library Cataloguing in Publication Data

Dunn, Douglas
Selected poems: 1964–1983.
I. Title
821'.914   PR6054.U54

ISBN 0–571–14619–8
ISBN 0–571–14620–1 Pbk

Library of Congress Cataloging-in-Publication Data

Dunn, Douglas.
Selected poems, 1964–1983.

I. Title.
PR6054.U54A6 1986   821'.914   86-16720
ISBN 0–571–14619–8
ISBN 0–571–14620–1 (pbk.)

Contents

LOVE OR NOTHING

from Terry Street

The Clothes Pit

The young women are obsessed with beauty.
Their old-fashioned sewing machines rattle in Terry
  Street.
They must keep up, they must keep up.

They wear teasing skirts and latest shoes,
Lush, impermanent coats, American cosmetics.
But they lack intellectual grooming.

In the culture of clothes and little philosophies,
They only have clothes. They do not need to be seen
Carrying a copy of *International Times*,

Or the Liverpool Poets, the wish to justify their looks
With things beyond themselves. They mix up colours,
And somehow they are often fat and unlovely.

They don't get high on pot, but get sick on cheap
Spanish Burgundy, or beer in rampant pubs,
And come home supported and kissed and bad-tempered.

But they have clothes, bright enough to show they dream
Of places other than this, an inarticulate paradise,
Eating exotic fowl in sunshine with courteous boys.

Three girls go down the street with the summer wind.
The litter of pop rhetoric blows down Terry Street,
Bounces past their feet, into their lives.

New Light on Terry Street

First sunshine for three weeks, and children come out
From their tents of chairs and old sheets,

Living room traffic jams, and battlefields of redcoat soldiers,
To expand, run on unsteady legs in and out of shades.

Up terraces of slums, young gum-chewing mothers sit
Outside on their thrones of light. Their radios,

Inside or placed on window ledges, grow hot
With sun and electricity. Shielding their eyes from sun

They talk above music, knitting or pushing prams
Over gentle, stone inches. Under clawed chairs

Cats sleep in the furry shade. Children bounce balls
Up into their dreams of sand, and the sea they have not seen.

Becoming tired, the fascination of wheels takes them.
They pedal their trikes slowly through dust in hollows,

Quietly give up cheek to old men, sing with sly voices.
A half-heard love song idles on the wind.

Yet there is no unrest. The dust is so fine.
You hardly notice you have grown too old to cry out for
change.

The Patricians

In small backyards old men's long underwear
Drips from sagging clotheslines.
The other stuff they take in bundles to the Bendix.

There chatty women slot their coins and joke
About the grey unmentionables absent.
The old men weaken in the steam and scratch at their
    rough chins.

Suppressing coughs and stiffnesses, they pedal bikes
On low gear slowly, in their faces
The effort to be upright, a dignity

That fits inside the smell of aromatic pipes.
Walking their dogs, the padded beats of pocket watches,
Muffled under ancient overcoats, silence their hearts.

They live watching each other die, passing each other
In their white scarves, too long known to talk,
Waiting for the inheritance of the oldest, a right to power.

The street's patricians, they are ignored.
Their anger proves something, their disenchantments
Settle round me like a cold fog.

They are the individualists of our time.
They know no fashions, copy nothing but their minds.
Long ago, they gave up looking in mirrors.

Dying in their sleep, they lie undiscovered.
The howling of their dogs brings the sniffing police,
Their middle-aged children from the new estates.

[5]

Men of Terry Street

They come in at night, leave in the early morning.
I hear their footsteps, the ticking of bicycle chains,
Sudden blasts of motorcycles, whimpering of vans.
Somehow I am either in bed, or the curtains are drawn.

This masculine invisibility makes gods of them,
A pantheon of boots and overalls.
But when you see them, home early from work
Or at their Sunday leisure, they are too tired

And bored to look long at comfortably.
It hurts to see their faces, too sad or too jovial.
They quicken their step at the smell of cooking,
They hold up their children and sing to them.

Incident in the Shop

Not tall, her good looks unstylized,
She wears no stockings, or uses cosmetic.

I sense beneath her blouse
The slow expanse of unheld breasts.

I feel the draughts on her legs,
The nip of cheap detergent on her hands.

Under her bed, forgotten winter bulbs
Die of thirst, in the grip of a wild dust.

Her husband beats her. Old women
Talk of it behind her back, watching her.

She buys the darkest rose I ever saw
And tucks its stem into her plastic belt.

A Removal from Terry Street

On a squeaking cart, they push the usual stuff,
A mattress, bed ends, cups, carpets, chairs,
Four paperback westerns. Two whistling youths
In surplus US Army battle-jackets
Remove their sister's goods. Her husband
Follows, carrying on his shoulders the son
Whose mischief we are glad to see removed,
And pushing, of all things, a lawnmower.
There is no grass in Terry Street. The worms
Come up cracks in concrete yards in moonlight.
That man, I wish him well. I wish him grass.

On Roofs of Terry Street

Television aerials, Chinese characters
In the lower sky, wave gently in the smoke.

Nest-building sparrows peck at moss,
Urban flora and fauna, soft, unscrupulous.

Rain drying on the slates shines sometimes.
A builder is repairing someone's leaking roof.

He kneels upright to rest his back.
His trowel catches the light and becomes precious.

From the Night-Window

The night rattles with nightmares.
Children cry in the close-packed houses,
A man rots in his snoring.
On quiet feet, policemen test doors.
Footsteps become people under streetlamps.
Drunks return from parties,
Sounding of empty bottles and old songs.
Young women come home
And disappear into white beds
At the edge of the night.
All windows open, this hot night,
And the sleepless, smoking in the dark,
Making small red lights at their mouths,
Count the years of their marriages.

Sunday Morning Among the Houses of
Terry Street

On the quiet street, Saturday night's fag-packets,
Balls of fish and chip newspaper, bottles
Placed neatly on window sills, beside cats.

A street of oilstains and parked motorbikes,
Wet confectionery wrappers becoming paste,
Things doing nothing, ending, rejected.

Revellers return tieless, or with hairdos deceased,
From parties, paying taxis in the cold,
Unsmiling in the fogs of deflated mirth.

Neighbours in pyjamas watch them from upstairs,
Chewing on pre-breakfast snacks,
Waiting for kettles to boil, wives quit the lav.

Men leave their beds to wash and eat,
Fumble with Sunday papers and radio knobs,
Leaving in their beds their wives and fantasies,

In bedside cups their teeth, their smiles.
Drinkers sleep into a blank sobriety,
Still talking to the faces in the smoke,

Women they regretted they were too drunk to touch,
Sucking tastes in their mouths, their mossy teeth.
Into the street come early-risen voices,

The Salvation Army's brass dulled in sunlessness
And breath of singers the colour of tubas.
Dog obbligatos rise from warm corners.

Behind the houses, antique plumbing
Coughs and swallows Sunday morning's flush
Down to Hull's underworld, its muddy roots.

A city of disuse, a sink, a place,
Without people it would be like the sea-bottom.
Beneath the street, a thundering of mud.

After Closing Time

Here they come, the agents of rot,
The street tarts and their celebrating trawlermen,
Singing or smoking, carrying bottles,
In a staggered group ten minutes before snow.

Winter

Recalcitrant motorbikes;
Dog-shit under frost; a coughing woman;
The old men who cannot walk briskly groaning
On the way back from their watchmen's huts.

Young Women in Rollers

Because it's wet, the afternoon is quiet.
Children, pacified with sweets inside
Their small houses, stroke travelling cats
From the kingdom of dustbins and warm smells.

Young women come to visit their married friend.
Waiting for their hair to set beneath thin scarves,
They walk about in last year's fashions,
Stockingless, in coats and old shoes.

They look strong, white-legged creatures
With nothing to do but talk of what it is to love
And sing words softly to the new tunes,
The type who burst each other's blackheads

In the street and look in handbag mirrors
While they walk, not talking of the weather,
Who call across the street they're not wearing knickers,
But blush when they pass you alone.

This time they see me at my window, among books,
A specimen under glass, being protected,
And laugh at me watching them.
They minuet to Mozart playing loudly

On the afternoon Third. They mock me thus,
They mime my culture. A landlord stares.
All he has worked for is being destroyed.
The slum rent-masters are at one with Pop.

The movements they imagine go with minuet
Stay patterned on the air. I can see soot,
It floats. The whiteness of their legs has changed
Into something that floats, become like cloth.

They disappear into the house they came to visit.
Out of the open door rush last year's hits,
The music they listen to, that takes up their time
In houses that are monuments to entertainment.

I want to be touched by them, know their lives,
Dance in my own style, learn something new.
At night, I even dream of ideal communities.
Why do they live where they live, the rich and the poor?

Tonight, when their hair is ready, after tea,
They'll slip through laws and the legs of policemen.
I won't be there, I'll be reading books elsewhere.
There are many worlds, there are many laws.

The Silences

It is urban silence, it is not true silence.
The main road, growling in the distance,
Continuous, is absorbed into it;
The birds, their noises become lost in it;
Faint, civilized music decorates it.

These are edges round a quiet centre where lives are lived,
Children brought up, where television aerial fixers come,
Or priests on black bikes to lecture the tardy.
If you turn your back on it, people are only noises,
Coughs, footsteps, conversations, hands working.

They are a part of the silence of places,
The people who live here, working, falling asleep,
In a place removed one style in time outwith
The trend of places. They are like a lost tribe.
Dogs bark when strangers come, with rent books, or
    free gifts.

They move only a little from where they are fixed.
Looking at worn clothes, they sense impermanence.
They have nothing to do with where they live, the silence
    tells them.
They have looked at it so long, with such disregard,
It is baked now over their eyes like a crust.

A Window Affair

We were looking at the same things,
Men on bikes, the litter round the drain,
The sparrows eating in the frozen shade.

We heard the same inweave of random noise,
The chant of children's games, and waiting cars
Of salesmen and collectors ticking over.

This was weekday flirtation, through the glass,
The love of eyes and silence, in which you cannot touch
Or talk, a useless love for the bored and tired.

Her window caught the winter sun and shone.
I imagined everything, the undressing, love,
The coy sleep. But there was nothing to say.

There were two faces, and they passed each other
Like shillings in circulation. Untouchable,
She was far away, in a world of foul language,

Two children, the television set in the corner,
As common as floral wallpaper or tea,
Her husband in at six to feed the greyhounds.

I used to crave the ideal life of Saturdays and Sundays,
A life of everything in a gay, short-lived country
Of high-living among the northern bricks,

Where people come out rested into the rain,
Wearing smiles as if they were expensive clothes,
Their bodies clean and warm and their jobs indoors.

But some ideals have passed far out of my reach,
The goodwill became full of holes like a sieve.
I grasp only the hard things, windows, contempt.

I could not kiss that face, the glowing mask
Of those who have been too much entertained,
That laughs the sour laugh and smells of food.

It's come to this, that in this time, this place,
There is a house I feel I have to leave,
Because my life is cracked, and in a room

Stares out of windows at a window face,
Thin shifts of dust on the sunning glass,
And does not want to love, and does not care.

Envoi

Why did I bring you to this Hull,
This rancid and unbeautiful
Surprise of damp and Englishness?
Mad for an education, for poetry,
I studied at our window,
My mind dying in shy cadences.
What cost of life was there, in poverty,
In my outlaw depressions, in your coping
With lonely, studious bohemia!

Now I choose to remember
Bus-rides together into Holderness,
Exploring the hedgerowed heat
On country walks by fields of mustard.
That view was broad and circular
Where everywhere seemed everywhere!

A curse on me I did not write with joy.

(1981)

The Worst of All Loves

Where do they go, the faces, the people seen
In glances and longed for, who smile back
Wondering where the next kiss is coming from?

They are seen suddenly, from the top decks of buses,
On railway platforms at the tea machine,
When the sleep of travelling makes us look for them.

A whiff of perfume, an eye, a hat, a shoe,
Bring back vague memories of names,
Thingummy, that bloke, what's-her-name.

What great thing have I lost, that faces in a crowd
Should make me look at them for one I know,
What are faces that they must be looked for?

But there's one face, seen only once,
A fragment of a crowd. I know enough of her.
That face makes me dissatisfied with myself.

Those we secretly love, who never know of us,
What happens to them? Only this is known.
They will never meet us suddenly in pleasant rooms.

Tribute of a Legs Lover

They are my dancing girls, the wasted lives,
The chorus girls who do not make good,
Who are not given flower shops or Schools of Dance
By rich and randy admirers, or marry
A gullible Joe from Swindon or Goole,
But find themselves stiff and rotten at fifty,
With bad legs, and no money to pay for the taxi,
Outside cheap drinking places on Grand National day.

Close of Play

Cricketers have the manners of ghosts,
Wandering in white on the tended ground.

They go in now, walking in twos and threes.
This sight is worth a week of evenings.

Players' wives and girlfriends put away tea-flasks,
Start complaining of goosepimples.

Nearby, the vicious pluck of unseen tennis,
A harrier contesting the park its contours,

Fighting a hill with rhythmic blue shoes.
Behind the trees, toughminded fops

In sports cars roar like a mini-Bacchus,
Their girls toss back their summer hair.

The sweet-smelling suburbs cool, settle.
Their people hesitate in the gap before night.

Now it is getting dark, they go indoors.
They do not dance by firelight on their lawns.

Inside, daughters practise one last scale,
Sober sons of teachers learn another fact.

Armchairs surround the tired, the lustful
Absorb their beds. On the garden table,

In the unrotting glasses, dregs of whisky
Or Martini become alive, golden smells.

Gardens aspire to wildness in the dark,
The cricket fields grow defiantly, reach up,

Trees become less polite. The groundsman's roller
Tries to crash screaming into the pavilion.

Out of the webs of ivy, silent as smoke,
Comes the wildness of the always growing,

The menace of unplanned shoots, the brick-eaters.
From taps and cisterns, water, the wild country,

Flows through bungalows and villas.
Damp corners grow moss. The golf course

Becomes a desert, a place without manners.
Rapists gather under hedges and bridges.

Horses in a Suburban Field

The road-dust settles behind the hedges
That enclose the small suburban fields.
Trees stand in straight lines, planted
By noblemen with an eye for order,
Trees in a park sold off to pay death duty.
Discarded things rot on the ground,
Paper shifts in the wind, metals rust.
Children play in the grass, like snakes,
Out of the way, on headache-soothing absences.

Sad and captured in a towny field,
The horses peep through the light,
Step over the tin cans, a bicycle frame.
They stand under a dried-up hawthorn
With dust on its leaves, smell distant kitchens.
Then they wander through the dust,
The dead dreams of housewives.

Love Poem

I live in you, you live in me;
We are two gardens haunted by each other.
Sometimes I cannot find you there,
There is only the swing creaking, that you have just left,
Or your favourite book beside the sundial.

A Dream of Judgement

Posterity, thy name is Samuel Johnson.
You sit on a velvet cushion on a varnished throne
Shaking your head sideways, saying No,
Definitely no, to all the books held up to you.
Licking your boots is a small Scotsman
Who looks like Boswell, but is really me.
You go on saying No, quite definitely no,
Adjusting the small volume of Horace
Under your wig and spitting in anger
At the portrait of Blake Swift is holding up.
Quite gently, Pope ushers me out into the hell
Of forgotten books. Nearby, teasingly,
In the dustless heaven of the classics,
There is singing of morals in Latin and Greek.

Landscape with One Figure

Shipyard cranes have come down again
To drink at the river, turning their long necks
And saying to their reflections on the Clyde,
'How noble we are.'

The fields are waiting for them to come over.
Trees gesticulate into the rain,
The nerves of grasses quiver at their tips.
Come over and join us in the wet grass!

The wings of gulls in the distance wave
Like handkerchiefs after departing emigrants.
A tug sniffs up the river, looking like itself.
Waves fall from their small heights on river mud.

If I could sleep standing, I would wait here
For ever, become a landmark, something fixed
For tug crews or seabound passengers to point at,
An example of being a part of a place.

South Bank of the Humber

Brickworks, generators of cities, break up
And then descend, sustaining no wages.

A sheet of corrugated iron smacks against a wall,
The wing of a pre-biological, inorganic bird.

It is the laughter of permanence,
The laughter of metal in a brickfield becoming dust.

The Queen of the Belgians

Commemorating Astrid's death
The Belgians made a postage stamp
That my father prized, for her face
Like my mother's, Thirties-beautiful,
Serene around its edges.

I've got it in my album now,
A thing handed down, like advice,
For me to find in the face
Of a queen at Europe's edge
What it was my father found.

Queen Astrid, that my father
Put in an album for her face,
Is puffed into my thoughts by love.
It beats there like the heart of all I know.
I am the age my father was.

Ships

When a ship passes at night on the Clyde,
Swans in the reeds, picking oil from their feathers,
Look up at the lights, the noise of new waves,
Against hill-climbing houses, malefic cranes.

A fine rain attaches itself to the ship like skin.
Lascars play poker, the Scottish mate looks
At the last lights, one that is Ayrshire,
Others on lonely rocks, or clubfooted peninsulas.

They leave restless boys without work in the river towns.
In their houses are fading pictures of fathers ringed
Among ships' complements in wartime, model destroyers,
Souvenirs from uncles deep in distant engine rooms.

Then the boys go out, down streets that look on water.
They say, 'I could have gone with them,'
A thousand times to themselves in the glass cafés,
Over their American soft drinks, into their empty hands.

A Poem in Praise of the British

Regiments of dumb gunners go to bed early.
Soldiers, sleepy after running up and down
Hideaway British Army meadows,
Clean the daisies off their mammoth boots.
The general goes pink in his bath reading
Lives of the Great Croquet Players.
At Aldershot, beside foot-stamping squares,
Young officers drink tea and touch their toes.

Heavy rain everywhere washes up the bones of British.
Where did all that power come from, the wish
To be inert, but rich and strong, to have too much?
Where does glory come from, and when it's gone
Why are old soldiers sour and the banks empty?
But how sweet is the weakness after Empire
In the garden of a flat, safe country shire,
Watching the beauty of the random, spare, superfluous,

Drifting as if in sleep to the ranks of memorialists
That wait like cabs to take us off down easy street,
To the redcoat armies, and the flags and treaties
In marvellous archives, preserved like leaves in books.
The archivist wears a sword and clipped moustache.
He files our memories, more precious than light,
To be of easy access to politicians of the Right,
Who now are sleeping, like undertakers on black cushions,

Thinking of inflammatory speeches and the adoring mob.
What a time this would be for true decadence!
Walking, new-suited, with trim whiskers, swinging
Our gold-knobbed walking sticks, to the best restaurants;
Or riding in closed black carriages to discreet salons,
To meet the women made by art, the fashionably beautiful;
Or in the garden, read our sonnets by the pool,
Beside small roses, next week's buttonholes.

In this old country, we are falling asleep, under clouds
That are like wide-brimmed hats. This is just right.
Old pederasts on the Brighton promenade
Fall asleep to dream of summer seductions.
The wind blows their hats away, and they vanish
Into archives of light, where greatness has gone,
With the dainty tea cup and the black gun,
And dancing dragoons in the fields of heaven.

Cosmologist

There is something joyful
In the stones today,
An inorganic ringing
At the roots of people.

The back of my hand
With its network of small veins
Has changed to the underside of a leaf.
If water fell on me now
I think I would grow.

from The Happier Life

The River Through the City

The river of coloured lights, black stuff
The tired city rests its jewels on.
Bad carnival, men and women
Drown themselves under the bridges.
Death-splash, and after, the river wears
The neon flowers of suicides.
Prints of silence ripple where they went in.
An old man rows a black boat and slides past
Unnoticed, a god in an oilskin coat.
He feeds the uncatchable black fish.
They know where Hitler is hiding.
They know the secrets behind sordid events
In Central Europe, in America and Asia,
And who is doing what for money.
They keep files on petty thieves, spies,
Adulterers and their favourite bureaucrats.
That's one old man who's nobody's uncle.
That's one fish you don't want with your chips.
Iron doors bang shut in the sewers.

The Friendship of Young Poets

There must have been more than just one of us,
But we never met. Each kept in his world of loss
The promise of literary days, the friendship
Of poets, mysterious, that sharing of books
And talking in whispers in crowded bars
Suspicious enough to be taken for love.

We never met. My youth was as private
As the bank at midnight, and in its safety
No talking behind backs, no one alike enough
To be pretentious with and quote lines at.

There is a boat on the river now, and
Two young men, one rowing, one reading aloud.
Their shirt sleeves fill with wind, and from the oars
Drop scales of perfect river like melting glass.

Nights of Sirius

Unknown men tonight will put
One last hand to a life's work,
Hobbyhorse or a pedantic search
For private seriousness;
Or add a wise last paragraph
To the privately published
Volume of family history,
Put back on the cherished shelf
Of an eccentric library
To be read in ten years' time
By a bookish grandson.

High summer, and dog-star nights
Are still and hot, accepting death
And notebooks, snapshot albums,
Treasured books and objects,
A chair, his favourite tie –
Possessions the dead have left,
What pleased them, passed their time,
And shall, like wives, preserve
Their marks of ownership,
Ways of what it felt like to be theirs,
Touch, pulse, the smell of hands.

The Musical Orchard

Girls on mopeds rode to Fécamp parties,
And as they passed the ripened orchard
Cheered an old man's music,
Not knowing it was sad.
Those French tunes on the saxophone,
The music inside fruit!

Backwaters

They are silent places, dilapidated cities
Obscure to the nation, their names spoken of
In the capital with distinct pejorative overtones.

For some, places mean coming to or going from,
Comedians and singers with their suitcases
Packed with signed photographs of themselves;

Businessmen in sharp suits, come to buy and sell,
Still seeking their paradise of transactions,
The bottomless market, where the mugs live.

For others, places are sites for existence,
Where roads slow down and come to a stop
Outside where it's good to be, particular places

Where instantly recognized people live,
The buses are a familiar colour and life is
Utterly civilian, all uniforms

Merely the kind insignia of postmen
And meter readers. There complacency means
Men are almost the same, and almost right.

And for a few, places are only the dumps
They end up in, backwaters, silent places,
The cheapest rooms of the cheapest towns.

These darker streets, like the bad days in our lives,
Are where the stutterers hide, the ugly and clubfooted,
The radically nervous who are hurt by crowds.

They love the sunlight at street corners
And the tough young men walking out of it,
And the police patrol. Poverty makes fools of them.

They have done so little they are hardly aware of themselves.
Unmissed, pensioned, at the far end of all achievements,
In their kiln-baked rooms, they are permanent.

Supreme Death

Fishing on a wide river from a boat
A corpse was caught, her black hair like a huge weed,
The hook stuck in a black shroud strangely marked.

There were others. Hundreds gathered round the boat,
Some turning, their white faces like pillows.
I lost my oars, and the river quickened.

On the towpath, men in their hundreds
Ran with the tide, singing, and pushing,
When they felt like it, some poor fool into the river.

Death, the best of all mysteries, layer
After layer is peeled off your secrecy
Until all that is left is an inexplicable ooze.

Too late, it is myself.
Too late, my heart is a beautiful top.
Too late, all the dead in the river are my friends.

Billie 'n' Me

You could never have been a friend of mine,
Even if I played as sweet as dead Lester
Three feet from you, because you mean too much,
Your voice opens all doors on fed-up love.

There were dreams of you, in the ideal night club,
The members gone, just you, the band, and me
In my white tuxedo resisting requests to leave,
Then walking back to my pampered hotel room

In a dawn of fanciful New York heights,
Wondering how you'd take my roses sent at noon,
The invitation to lunch, that you ignored,
The lyrics I had written but you would not sing,

Black, dead, put down by love that was too much,
Mismanaged pleasures. And silent now
As the saxophones in Harlem pawnshops,
Your voice that meant how tough love is.

Midweek Matinée

The lunch hour ends and men go back to work,
Plumbers with long bags, whistling office boys
With soup on their ties and pee on their shoes,
Typists with a sandwich and a warm coke.

The indolent or lucky are going to the cinema.
There too go the itinerant heavy drinkers,
Who take the piss out of bus conductors
Or fall asleep in public reading rooms

Over unlikely learned periodicals.
They come in late, just after closing time,
And sprawl in the cheap front seats
Dressed in the raincoats of a thousand wet nights,

Muttering with the lips of the unknown kisses.
Legendary, undeserving drunks, beggarly
And good for pity or laughter, you show
What happens to men who are not good at life,

Where happiness is demanded and lives are lived
For entertainment. I watch you sleep,
Grey humps in an empty cinema. You're dangerous.
All wish you were not there, cramping the style.

You are very bad, you are worse than civilized,
Untouched by seriousness or possessions,
Treading the taxpayers' roads, being found
Incapable in public places, always hungry,

Totally unlike what people should be – washed,
Happy, occupied, idle only in snatches
Of paid-for amusement or cynical truancies.
You have cut yourself off from barbers and supermarkets.

I don't want you here on my page, pink faces
Under spit and stubble, as fools or martyrs.
You are not new, you have nothing to sell.
You are walking evictions. You have no rentbooks.

You never answer telephones or give parties.
If you have a sense of humour, I want to know.
You claim the right to be miserable
And I can't stand what you bring out into the open.

The Hunched

They will not leave me, the lives of other people.
I wear them near my eyes like spectacles.
Sullen magnates, hunched into chins and overcoats
In the back seats of their large cars;
Scholars, so conscientious, as if to escape
Things too real, names too easily read,
Preferring language stuffed with difficulties;
And children, furtive with their own parts;
A lonely glutton in the sunlit corner
Of an empty Chinese restaurant;
A coughing woman, leaning on a wall,
Her wedding-ring finger in her son's cold hand,
In her back the invisible arch of death.
What makes them laugh, who lives with them?

I stooped to lace a shoe, and they all came back,
Mysterious people without names or faces,
Whose lives I guess about, whose dangers tease.
And not one of them has anything at all to do with me.

Emblems

Rich nights in another climate –
White tables and the best Moselle,
A garden that slopes to a clear river;
Style I cannot make and was not born to claim.

And the factory is humming at full production
Just over the hill, making money,
Whispering, a big fish without eyes,
The most profound unhappiness.

The Sportsmen

Scum, they have fast cars and money
And take other men's wives to play tennis.

They are always with us, making us laugh
At parties, in the pub. They live for prowess,

To be good at pastimes. Their times will come.
An ordinary man will beat them at their favourite games,

They will be murdered in bedrooms,
Their cars pressed into squares of scrap.

After the War

The soldiers came, brewed tea in Snoddy's field
Beside the wood from where we watched them pee
In Snoddy's stagnant pond, small boys hidden
In pines and firs. The soldiers stood or sat
Ten minutes in the field, some officers apart
With the select problems of a map. Before,
Soldiers were imagined, we were them, gunfire
In our mouths, most cunning local skirmishers.
Their sudden arrival silenced us. I lay down
On the grass and saw the blue shards of an egg
We'd broken, its warm yolk on the green grass,
And pine cones like little hand grenades.

One burst from an imaginary Browning,
A grenade well thrown by a child's arm,
And all these faces like our fathers' faces
Would fall back bleeding, trucks would burst in flames,
A blood-stained map would float on Snoddy's pond.
Our ambush made the soldiers laugh, and some
Made booming noises from behind real rifles
As we ran among them begging for badges,
Our plimsolls on the fallen May-blossom
Like boots on the faces of dead children.
But one of us had left. I saw him go
Out through the gate, I heard him on the road
Running to his mother's house. They lived alone,
Behind a hedge round an untended garden
Filled with broken toys, abrasive loss;
A swing that creaked, a rusted bicycle.
He went inside just as the convoy passed.

Modern Love

It is summer, and we are in a house
That is not ours, sitting at a table
Enjoying minutes of a rented silence,
The upstairs people gone. The pigeons lull
To sleep the under-tens and invalids,
The tree shakes out its shadows to the grass,
The roses rove through the wilds of my neglect.
Our lives flap, and we have no hope of better
Happiness than this, not much to show for love
Than how we are, or how this evening is,
Unpeopled, silent, and where we are alive
In a domestic love, seemingly alone,
All other lives worn down to trees and sunlight,
Looking forward to a visit from the cat.

Guerrillas

They lived on farms, were stout and freckled, knew
Our country differently, from work, not play.
Fathers or brothers brought them to school in cars,
Dung on the doors, fresh eggs in the back.
The teachers favoured them for their wealth,
Daffodils and free eggs, and we envied them
The ownership of all the land we roved on,
Their dangerous dogs and stately horses,
The fruit we had to steal, their land being
Income, and ours a mysterious provider.
They owned the shadows cast by every branch,
Chestnuts and flowers, water, the awkward wire.
Their sullen eyes demanded rent, and so
We shouted the bad words to their sisters,
Threw stones at hens, blocked up the froggy drains.
Outlaws from dark woods and quarries,
We plundered all we envied and had not got,
As if the disinherited from farther back
Came to our blood like a knife to a hand.

Under the Stone

They sleep out the day in Grimsby, Goole, or Hull,
The sleep of Empire sherry and unspeakable liquors,
And clumsily beg at the Saturday cinema queues
From steady workers and their penny-pinching girlfriends,
The washed and sober, who only want to laugh or listen.

These men remind them of the back of their minds.
Splendid barbarians, they form tribes in the slums
Up certain dim streets, the tribes of second-hand,
In empty houses no one wants to buy,
Abandoned rooms the poor have given up.

No one wants to see them, in a grey dawn, walk down
The empty streets, an army of unkept appointments,
Broken promises, irregular meal times,
Portents of bad harvests and unemployment,
Cavalry in the streets, and children shouting 'Bread! Bread!'

But they mean nothing, they live under the stone.
They are their own failures and our nightmares
Or longings for squalor, the bad meanings we are.
They like it like that. It makes them happy,
Walking the rubble fields where once houses were.

The New Girls

Dancing and drinking go on into the night
In rooms of Edwardian houses,
In flats that cads and fashionable young couples rent,
Where Saturday's parties happen
After the pub everyone goes to has closed.

There are always the girls there no one's seen before,
Who soon become known and their first names
    remembered,
Replacing the girls who 'simply just vanished'
To new jobs in London or husbands who've quietened
    down.
The new girls leave with the men who brought them

To rooms nearby in the same district, or one just like it.
At dawn, three streets from their homes,
The girls leave cars with doors that slam,
Engines that sound like men's contemptuous laughter,
As they disappear at fifty down an empty street.

Then they reach the door, and turn the key, and know
They have been listening to their own footsteps
In the silence of Sunday before the milkmen,
When the cats are coming home to eat, and water dripping
From the bridge is heard a hundred yards away.

Saturday Night Function

The cinemas empty, and backs of seats
Become varnished waves, the light ordinary.

Solemn couples go through the coat routine,
Check for gloves, cigarette case, spectacles.

First out, the fat boys glide to their doorways
To eat double fish and chips and watch the thin

Ushers lead out the sleepy old men.
The happy couples are already miles away.

Seducers, anxious for this week's insert,
Their hands warming in shiny black gloves,

Have hailed black patent leather taxis
And taken the girl to a flat in the suburbs.

The other style are out in the country,
Love among the spanners in ample vans.

Bored narcissists, for whom friendship is an ache,
Look for themselves in bus-queues and railway stations.

Stylish youths speed to parties
Intent on any wildness that doesn't make you fat

And you don't have to pay for. Lonely drunks
Collide with the respectable, begging their pardons.

In the city rhythm of the last bus home
Is where I come in, imagining the night

[55]

Of four hundred thousand lives,
A man bleeding after a brawl,

A child with toothache after too much cake.
Night after night, the same sleep, machines,

Wheels, lights, still alive when the lives rest,
The silence after entertainment.

from Love or Nothing

The House Next Door

Old dears gardening in fur coats
And 'Hush Puppies', though it's a mild July,
Once met Freddie Lonsdale at John o' Groats.
Their keyboard's Chopin and their humour's wry.
   There's no one I'd rather be called 'famous' by.
   They have an antique goldfish, a cat called Sly.

They live in my unpublished play
For two sad characters. Their Chippendale
Haunts England's salesrooms, their silver tray
That brought Victoria's breakfast and her mail.
   I visit their house – its coffee aroma,
   The cat out cold in its afternoon coma!

I watch them watching for the post,
Wondering who writes. In *my* play, no one writes,
They are alone, together, and have lost
Our century by being old. Their nights
   Are spent rehearsing through Irving Berlin;
   The gardens turn to stage-sets when they begin.

My best times with them are 'Chopin
Mornings'. They smile vainly at my small applause –
No one plays the Pole as badly as they can –
And Sly stands up, and purrs, stretching his claws,
   Playing his cat's piano on the cushions,
   And called by pianist sisters, Perfect Nuisance.

There garage is pronounced gar*age*,
Strawberries never known as strawbs, but *fraises*,
And cheddar is called cheese, the rest *fromage*,
And all life is a lonely Polonaise.
    Why do I love them, that milieu not mine,
    The youngest, laughingly, 'last of the line'?

No answers. They have given me
Too much for answering. I am their pet,
Like Sly. They have defied me, cutting free
From my invention. 'Let us live. Forget
    You made us up for money. We'll give you tea,
    And you shall drive our ancient crock down to the sea.'

Winter Graveyard

Mossed obelisks and moss-gloved curves,
Uncherishable headstones
Rise from the dead place at a time of death.
A swarm of fissured angels sweeps over
Unremarkable civilians,
Magnates of no inheritance;
In depths of briar and ivy
Their utterly negative remains –
Dried convolvulus,
A bush of nerves sprouted
From lost anatomies.

Survivors of scattered families
Can't get at inscriptions.
When did Frederick die? Or Emily?
They need to know. Relatives
Underfoot impart a sad feeling
Worth expeditions
Sometimes beaten back by the strength
Of wild entanglements
Pensioners declare is neglect, unprincipled
Spite of generation for generation,
And imply their own regret.

How can they bear to know they are
Now similarly fated
In a city not even a metropolis,
And their cross a broken ornament?
Even that era of grand proprieties,
Domain of the picture-hook and claw-footed table,
Its offering servants,
Is sunk and forgotten,
Submerged under midget Gothic.
Fast sycamores grow
Upright out of Victorian creeper.

This is a door to Victoria's heaven.
Sinking one's face in a cushion,
Sharing, as if from an alms box,
Love preserved in Death,
And its hundred-thousand sentiments –
The man who came from the house
With the dancers to talk of the summer,
A soldier who told Edwardian merchants
Of a minor campaign in Assam.
They dance now to secret ragtime
In red-plush joints.

Once they were blue citizenry
At the ends of streets, in horse-traffic.
If I shut my eyes
They are still there, in the same stillness,
The same harmonious dusk
Of a generation whose male children –
Young in 1914 –
Are not buried here
But died abroad defending an Empire's
Affectionate stability
And an industry of lies.

Rank everlastingness
Mud-buttered –
Money is this,
One old penny at the edge of a grave,
Shrill starlings over
Columns and sarcophagi, as many as
The corners hiding God
Here, in his formal dump.
Rubbish of names under vomit of moss;
Inscriptions incised
In thin velvet

Rinse their loving vocabularies
In the light of dreams.
And I am momentarily disabled by
The thought that this is real – pink sky
Behind the black upreaching trees,
Aspirations of beauty and love
Disregarding corroded vulgarity
And farcical monuments
To sanctities not worth the enshrinement
That outlast memory and money.
And a white bird leaves a bare tree.

Winter Orchard

Five days of fog over snow,
Thinning, thickening, thinning
Before dark,
Its last substantial grit,
A breath with industry on it.

Blank miseries
Of the average dead;
Miscellaneous, unspectacular visitation;
Spiritual dregs
Out of the gutters of what-drab-Heaven,

The City of what-suburbanly-managerial-God?
Cold torpor of questions,
Revenge of the unfructified,
Yesterday,
The ash that looks like air.

Emerging, sailing,
Unrescuable grey-drenched browns
Of unpruned apple trees,
Their crush of twigs,
Threat of unleafed forks . . .

An apple is still stuck there,
Almost yellow in this light.
One survivor of harvest;
Unreachable,
It flourished but came to nothing.

Best efforts are negative,
Seriously beautiful, like art.
Clear light speaks valediction;
Sparse branches
In an orchard of goodbyes,

So many lines that spume or trail off
Beyond limits, their own reaches.
The sky is a net of black nerves,
Continued dream-lines of trees.
Fog's majesty,

Sheer strength of numbers, departs;
Swish of moth-eaten cloaks,
Coarse garments –
Generation upon labouring generation
Of conscripts and grocers' assistants,

Millhands, the unnamed courtiers
Of long-dead industrial magnates.
Their souls shine
On wet slates in summer, sliced turn
Of an autumn furrow, a now-sacred pippin,

As the snow melts like white grease
And soot-spotted stalactites vanish
In their own directions
To destinations that are sounds and wetness;
A soft, cold world
That grows dark when fog clears,
The ground that receives the apple.

In the Small Hotel

There they must live for ever, under soft lights,
The cheated at their favourite separate tables,
Inactive thirds of tender adulteries.

They stare into a light that is always evening,
Their eyes divided, as if distracted by
The ghost of something only one eye sees

Sleep-walking in plastic darkness
Around the night-clubs. They sit like chessmen
At their linen squares, waiting to be moved.

No one makes conversation. A hand
May absently arrange roses in a vase
Or wave away the leering gypsy fiddler.

Chefs please no one there and the waiters stamp
Untipped among customers too vague and lost
Ever to think of coming back to commerce.

People we did not want or could not keep;
Someone did this to them, over and over,
Wanting their unhappiness until it happened.

Across the dewy grass with a small suitcase
Love comes trotting and stops to hold on a shoe.
To go away with *her*! To drive the limousine

With contraceptives in the glove compartment
Beside the chocolates and packaged orchid
And find that new Arcadia replacing Hollywood! –

Remote and amatory, a style of life
In which no one offends or intrudes.
They might as well live in their wardrobes.

The Global Fidget

'Miss E., so kind and clean, once Mrs S.,
But now "reverted back", as Miss E. says,
Is tidy at the picnic, holding wine.
She talks about her "loves", such anodyne
Remembrances, and can't help being trite.
But we excuse her faith – Miss E. is tight.

'Dear Edith Ermine, we once thought you brave.
That horseback expedition with a slave
You'd freed in Berbera inspired us through
Our teens. I had such high regard for you
In all my girlhood, and your postcards meant
Such satisfaction and such discontent,

'Still growing up straight-laced and bored
With school, dull friends, and the routinely-scored
And endless tennis. My friends were *not* dull;
By being gone, you made me act the fool,
Wanting to be with you, alive and far
Strolling that market place at Kandahar,

'And snapped with white-socked officers, and wooed
By potentates. Today the word is "screwed",
But you, prim mother's sister, my dear aunt,
Are broke and loveless, quite ignored, and can't,
For all your tales, disguise the fact that travel
Is nothing to experience, a drivel

'Of distance and an obstacle of seas
To cross and reach your trivial ecstacies.
And now, half cut, or "tipsy" as you say,
You woo my daughter with the midnight day
Of Lapland, followed by the Karroo heat,
Adventures in the Andamans. Dead beat

'Of expeditionary life, you roved,
I know. I'd love you for it, if you'd proved
Your own affections, given proof, just once,
Of selflessness, and love. And now the chance
Is that my daughter will grow up like me,
Wanting your sort of past, the rich and free

'Lady traveller of the China Seas,
Sister to warlords, nurse of missionaries.
Long-skirted, overland Herodotus,
Dear Edith, aunt, what will become of us?
You have successes, failures, like the rest,
And I am static. Your way of life is best?

'Broke and put up by disenchanted friends
Bored with your reminiscence of the ends
Of geography, you look forward to *us*,
Your complicated nieces, and our fuss
Of children, husbands, thinking that you please,
Opening the atlas of your memories.'

Realisms

(To Derek Mahon)

Poetry in a flap,
Its paper efficiencies,
Thoth with an accent.

Details shrug me off,
Rain from a wet coat;
I am shoulders.

You have the same concern;
The real stuff hurts, efforts
To write it down confuse,

Or soothe too much, having
Too many ideas to start with,
Too many words.

Whittling down
An algebra of 'sympathies'
Through brilliant sums

To a sudden Nothing,
We find a glimpse of housing estates,
A duster on a window

Waving to a street
Its goodbyes to the spirit
Of domestic energies.

At the moist limits
Of Zero, where worlds turn
Vegetable or wiry

And politics dissolve,
Gunfire is silent.
Its echo reached us here,

Far down in France, the thud
That hits the citizens who die
For random's cause –

The cause of being them,
Of being there, blown to pieces
As they drink their tea.

I am against most revolutions,
All conformities. You must demur.
At least, raise your eyebrows.

Nothing helps.
Our fatuous surrender
To the language deals

No impertinence or blow.
We puff our alphabets
Back to the oratorical soup

Of Ireland, Scotland,
To a thousand stabs in the back,
The inhabitants of opposition.

Our cities of shipyards,
Belfast, Glasgow, fervent closures
Of protestantism dispensed with –

We never escape them,
Returning to stale dreams,
Old possibilities, dismissed

In the eyes of generators
Of what we kicked from our heels,
And friends who stayed

To admonish our absences.
Streets, an altered skyline,
The half-remembered face

Of an early girlfriend
We might almost have married
Under the trees of the playground –

And the dream comes back,
Again and again, far away
At the ends of roads,

The existential clarity
Of love and nothing, the peace
Poets in patched trousers deserve.

Renfrewshire Traveller

Home rain, an aerial night-Clyde,
Spray of recollection
And my only appropriate welcome.

Have I come back?
It was dark
Through Kilmarnock,

Johnny Walker blinked
Imperfectly; history
Is whisky, *lacrimae rerum*.

Have I come back?
I am Scots, a tartan tin box
Of shortbread in a delicatessen of cheddars

And southern specialties.
I am full of poison.
Each crumb of me is a death,

Someone you never see again
After funerals in the rain.
Men who return wearing black ties,

Men who return having looked for work –
Hear them, their Glasgow accents
In the night of high-rise

Skyward tenements, railway platforms,
The accents of rain and arguments.
What have I come to?

Not this. Not this
Slow afright over rails,
This ache in a buffet of empty beer-cans.

This wiping of windows to see a city
Rise from its brilliant lack,
Its fixtures in transparent butter.

Not this visitor
To a place of relatives,
A place of names.

Unlucky Mariners

Clapped out, with long necks
And thin bodies pivoting
On paunches,
They sit like unstrung banjos
Waiting their names to be called.

I dream of rusting hulks
In the Indies,
Jammed among the mangrove
Where sea stops inch by inch,
Water, snakes and vegetable are one.

'John Rigg, you spilled your rum
From Stornoway to the dreary Plate.
I saw you wench Malacca
Under the palms;
You changed your ladies with the tide.'

Dance of the shingle resort,
Foreshore trash
And harbour-masters counting
Prosperity by tonnage –
Here are the makers of music,

The numbers missed by arithmetic,
Unshipped and down on their luck
As they have been down on their luck
In disgusting jails
Near all the harbours.

'MacBryde, you shipped out of Glasgow
In '32, and you're back
With five German duckings
And thoughts of as many bastards
As you've had slit-skirted slope-eyed whores.'

Once, on a raft on a lagoon
Of Renfrewshire's Clyde,
An old man waved from his freighter;
He had nothing to do but wave to me,
And I thought, 'I'll go to sea.'

I dream of rusting hulks
And undersea
The leaky tubs that God's torpedo
Plugged; in South Pacific huts
The lucky mariners, copra kings

With four wives and the respect
Of The Islands,
Playing much-repaired concertinas
Long into the night,
To the tropical stars.

And I look at this lot,
Calling out their names
From *The Ledger of Missing Seafarers*,
So seldom called
They think I call their fathers.

Their grey skins are radiant mist,
Their eyes deep pools
In which the monsters sleep –
From nautical boyhoods
To skeletal service on The Ghost Ship.

'Falkenberg, you've a lot
To answer for. Your slummy crew
Picked off the bobbing wrecks
Might answer to your bells
But you're shipless now.'

Wrecks of many seas,
Here by the silent shipyards
Of the shore, ghosts of nuts and bolts
Toast your epiphanies
In the transparent grave of the fish!

White Fields

An aeroplane, its red and green night-lights
Spotting its distant noise in the darkness;
'Jack Frost', you say, pointing to white fields
Sparkling. My eyes accept the dark, the fields
Extend, spreading and drifting, fences rising
Before the black hedge that zips beside the road
I'm told I must never try to cross without you.
'What time is it?' – 'The middle of the night!
You've had a dream, I heard you shout.'
It woke me and I cried aloud, until
My mother came and showed me the farm
Wasn't burning, the school still had its roof,
There was no one hidden in the little fir trees.
'Only an aeroplane!' – As if you meant
That there, in 1948 in Renfrewshire,
We were safe from fear, and the white eyes
Of dead Jews were just photographs
In a terrible past, a neighbour's magazine.
'Only an aeroplane!' Unsleeping factories,
All night you busied overhead, and flames
Flushed out my cities made of shoe-boxes
And dominoes, my native village of shaws.
Innocent machine! I had a toy like you
That I made buzz and drone like Leaper's bees,
From which I dropped the A-bomb on John's pram,
Crumpling the hand-embroidered sheets.

Our breath melted ice on the window-pane.
Fields drizzled on the glass, opening strips
Of short-lived clarity, and fingernails of ice
Slid to the sill. 'No harm will come to us.'
I slept. Till now I've slept, dreaming of mice
Burrowing under the crusted tufts of snow
That heaviest fall had left us with,
Our planet flooded into continents
Of stray, white islands, a sea too cold to swim.
Till now I've slept, and waking, I reject
Your generation, an old copy of *Everybody's*
Thrown out with *Film Fun* and the tea leaves,
Bulldozed by a conscript from our village
Into a pit dug by forced labour.
So easily is love shed, I hardly feel it.

White fields, your angled frost filed sharply
Bright over undisturbed grasses, do not soothe
As similes of innocence or idle deaths
That must happen anyway, an unmoral blankness;
Be unforgiving stillness, natural, what is:
Crimes uttered in landscape, smoke-darkened snow.

Trains in my distance altered. Cattle trucks
Seemed to chug through Georgetown, a station
Where a fat man in a black uniform kept hens
On the platform. The waggons sprouted arms
And dropped dung, and no one sang
'Ten Green Bottles' or 'The Sash.' Offensive outings.

Six years old! And I lived through the worst of it!

The Competition

When I was ten, going to Hamilton
On the Leyland bus named for Eddlewood,
A boy with an aeroplane just like mine
Zoomed at his war games in the seat in front.
I'd never seen such a school uniform –
As brown as the manure in Cousar's coup
Where someone's city cousin had jumped in
Having been told it was 'just sand' –
One of Glasgow's best fee-paying places,
Brown as barrowloads from the blue-bottled byre.
I couldn't help it; I had to talk to him
And tell him I, too, had a Hurricane.
His mother pulled him to her, he sat sullen,
As if I'd spoiled his game. I spoke again,
And he called me a poor boy, who should shut up.
I'd never thought of it like that.
The summer tenements were so dry I cried.
My grandfather wouldn't give *him* sixpence;
He'd never have a grudge as lovely as mine.

Years later, running in a race, barefooted
As I'd trained my spikes to ruin, convinced
My best competitor was him, I ran into
The worst weathers of pain, determined to win,
But on the last lap, inches from the tape, was beaten
By someone from Shotts Miners' Welfare Harriers Club.

Boys With Coats

When I was ten, outside the Govan Plaza,
My first day on the Glasgow Underground,
I gave a boy with no coat in the sleet and rain
My pocket-money and my model aeroplane.
He said he was going to Greenock, the place
For which our bus was named, 'via Inchinnan'
Where we lived in village comfort near
An aerodrome – HMS *Sanderling*,
Its concrete fields of war named for a bird
I'd never seen. 'My father's in Greenock,'
He said; but the conductress wouldn't let him on.
Faces through streaming windows stared contempt
To see him set off in the wet to Linthouse,
Where they all guessed he lived – the tenements
That frightened me because they were so dark.

I'd sat in Monty's staff car at the Motor Show,
Having been born on the night of Alamein
In the war that serving justice served injustice –
That boys with coats might give to those without,
Effacing rights of ownership with gifts.
And I felt radical, that my lost Hurricane
Solved nothing in the sleet and rain.

Sailing with the Fleet

Delivering potatoes on the sea
Seemed hardly naval. The skeleton crews
On parked destroyers waiting to be scrapped
Smoked by their mothballed guns. Our MFV
Shambled through the gusts towards the clapped
Out flagship with their grub, our galley brews
Hot in our hands, life-jacketed and gloved
Cadets in blue December, glabrous boys
Among hulk-veterans of the convoys,
She-ships their sailors probably had loved.

Two rusting *K.G. Five*-class battleships
Were tended by our spuds, twins of the two
The Japanese torpedoed off Malaya,
Our Jimmy said. Our unheroic trips,
Bill Haley on our wind-up record player,
Were less magnificent. One thousand blue
South China Sea deaths, and many sunk tons –
Dead relatives of these, whose listless ratings
Watched workmen cut away the awful guns.
Such rust-reminders. Such steel. Such waitings.

Clydesiders

Men in boiler-suits zip twice, Clyde-built.
Thirsts, you come to this, a gush against the Shanks,
Fag-ends in the urinal, Navy Cut
Of yellow leaf, little boats of Capstan
Along the trough, blue-bottles on a crust,
And down the drain, grey ash of smokers' silt.

My poems should be Clyde-built, crude and sure,
With images of those dole-deployed
To honour the indomitable Reds,
Clydesiders of slant steel and angled cranes;
A poetry of nuts and bolts, born, bred,
Embattled by the Clyde, tight and impure.

My footprints tread a rug of settled sawdust,
The carpentering corner of a Yard.
I made these marks, have gone back to London,
No victim of my place, but mad for it.
A shower of rain, my footprints melt and run.
They'll follow to my life. I know they must.

Caledonian Moonlight

The white moon opens over a ridge of bracken
Spilling its prodigal rays into the eyes
Of the last pair of wildcat in the county
Looking for the kittens of their sterility
In the wiry heather

And the beautiful white face of a secretary
Rises in the shut eyes of a bachelor caretaker
Whose mother is dreaming
Of handing a plate of sandwiches to the minister

There are more moons in the night
Than eyes of those who see them
Open, venereal

Going to Bed

Free as the frequent rain,
And our footprints rise from their deepest marks
Till the globe is smooth of us again.

'Mundus senescit' says my priest.
The world grows old in moonlight.
And more than that, the world was always old.

Love, who is warm?
Even at this hour, the motorbikes
Gurgle their vehemences,

All-night taxis huddle round the telephone,
Sonorous locomotives pull away from time
Into the night of may-blossom,

Night that subdues the verticals
And leaves the world flat, its floating lights
Pulsing, excited hearts of predators.

Once, to a girl, I said, 'Hell is hard.
Forget me. That's easy.' And was that bad?
But being bored is full of such surprises.

And now we fly, not mattering much,
And only then to you and I,
Pale ecstasisers in a glade of rooms

When just by looking we can see our minds
Or with our fingers turn the moon
Of this excited May, to see its other side,

The Apple-Island and our carnal truth
Hushed out of its confusion by
Physical orchards, slowed rush of waves.

I Am a Cameraman

They suffer, and I catch only the surface.
The rest is inexpressible, beyond
What can be recorded. You can't be them.
If they'd talk to you, you might guess
What pain is like though they might spit on you.

Film is just a reflection
Of the matchless despair of the century.
There have been twenty centuries since charity began.
Indignation is day-to-day stuff;
It keeps us off the streets, it keeps us watching.

Film has no words of its own.
It is a silent waste of things happening
Without us, when it is too late to help.
What of the dignity of those caught suffering?
It hurts me. I robbed them of privacy.

My young friends think Film will be all of Art.
It will be revolutionary proof.
Their films will not guess wrongly and will not lie.
They'll film what is happening behind barbed wire.
They'll always know the truth and be famous.

Politics softens everything.
Truth is known only to its victims.
All else is photographs – a documentary
The starving and the playboys perish in.
Life disguises itself with professionalism.

Life tells the biggest lies of all,
And draws wages from itself.
Truth is a landscape the saintly tribes live on,
And all the lenses of Japan and Germany
Wouldn't know how to focus on it.

Life flickers on the frame like beautiful hummingbirds.
That is the film that always comes out blank.
The painting the artist can't get shapes to fit.
The poem that shrugs off every word you try.
The music no one has ever heard.

The Concert
(For Peter Porter)

The last piano in the world
Is about to be played
In a room empty of all other furniture.
There are parts of the floor you cannot stand on.
These parts are called 'holes'.

The pianist has the last clean white shirt,
The last hale suit with tails.
Some people won't believe
Our sponsors found a piece of soap
For him to wash his hands.
But he has no shoes.
Alas, there are no longer any shoes.

And the room fills with people,
Apart from those parts called 'holes' in the old language.
But some stand on the ground, in the 'holes',
With their heads looking over the floorboards,
Through ragged trousers, women's legs.

Latecomers sit outside in the long grass,
Among the foxgloves, thick vines of ivy
That strangle the plains, playing with
Stale, blanched bones of the unfortunate.

The old ones of the audience
Anticipate the works of Bach,
Mozart, Scriabin, Beethoven,
Debussy, Chopin, Liszt.
They are just names to them,
Names that make them think, or hum
What was written by someone else.

And the pianist sits down,
And the people remember to clap.
Then the old pianist weeps.
For all he can remember
Is *Three Blind Mice*.

The White Poet

(Homage to Jules Laforgue)

I've travelled by the ice-floes
Purer than purest first white communicants.
I don't go to church . . .
I'm the High Chancellor of Insight,
Remember that . . .

I am a random harvest of cells,
Thinking, farting, married.
I could have been the perfect husband –
The whispering of her long dress over the carpet
In the next room is a magic hush-hush.

My shoes have walked cobblers' miles
On the backstreets. Rain, and spires of factories
In the rain . . . pianos in all the houses –
Agoraphobic furniture drizzle would love to warp.
The keyboard, an international gutter.

Pianos in the prim districts are playing
Tedious waltzes, the music of moderation.
And over the domes of swimming-baths
A clarinet's chalumeau tune drags from subterranean
   woods
Amazing possibilities of Priapus.

All Saints, Margaret Street, a wedding in a doorway
Touted by photographers, waiting for a cab . . .
Red-brick palace, streaming, baked,
Naked in its numbered days, hallowing the weddings
Of ill-dressed parties without taxis.

And the melancholy horns! Sad, undersea
Deranged tan-tivvy, dislocated fanfare!
Driven on the North Wind, ta-ra! ta-ta!
Turning the head of the groom who stands
Like a gland ripped from a throat.

Tanneries, chemical works, docks, post offices,
Brassy flourish of work, the diseased architecture –
Fog-flecked spittle solid on the soul.
Nature, stale factory of sap with the frenzied stink,
Is no one in love?

Or is *this* love?
All night, Our Lady of the Evenings
Never makes her mind up. Her leave-takings
Are the swishes of black dresses,
She loves a box of brutal adornments –

A gross Gothic of smoke and bubbling vats,
A Northern torch of furnaces
And Sunday afternoons of business districts
Evaporated of their carnal typists.
Hypochondria and slaughter!

Chattering in the streets, chattering in the shops,
Small talk of commercial companionships –
Where the corner-shop is an off-licence, the delicatessen
Is usually closed. That street is pretty.
This is what is meant by a City. That is the lesson.

And railway stations, breathless at the platform's end –
How lovely to look at, those trains we miss!
Gentlemen, lift the seat! Gone, without me!
Splendid, splendid, to leave the friend
Waiting with his watch in the specified pub.

Moon-woman, lover, I would gladly wring from you
White bodies of the populace
To save them, but you laugh,
Offering your ligature of nebulous caresses,
Pale oddities, mottoes of madness

And nothing to grab hold of. Moon, sick angel
Suspended through stages of globular striptease,
You vanish like love, the personality
Sipped through ice, the woman's lips on her Daiquiri –
Crushed, fragile pink drizzle in blankness.

God so loved the world
He puked every time he looked at it,
With a few miraculous exceptions. He's gone now.
Sundays, and parked cars of visitors, special joints
Like amputated stumps oozing in the ovens.

And it is the day of *The Moderation Waltz* –
   We will not buy the best, *one two three*
   We won't beat our breasts, *one two three*
   And we'll have no truck
   With that muck
   In foreign restaurants, *da-da dum-dum*

Paupers are swimming through their blood
To meet their other parents at the far end
Where fauntleroys picnic in stable sunshine
And father punts mother on the river
To the crystal honeymoon.

O waves of honey, Moon, perambulators, gloves!
Useless apostrophes!
The world is passionate as insomnia –
Insomnia of power stations sailing
In self-generated glows like bulky saints;

Insomnia of engines that start with a twist;
Insomnia of police forces, watching
Vulnerable depots of money;
Ships on their incessant stagger;
Insomniac clocks, hysterically

Ticking, the tick-tick-tock
And obliging semaphore
On the complaisant eye
Of the clock – punctual, early, late,
And remember you must die.

Sundays, time-locks, vaults, factories –
Over the land of Sunday, my wet love,
I stretch my hand.
What joins us is an ampersand.
It's easier for us. Should I take off my glove?

Should I cry in the streets, or sail over the rooftops –
Silver Street, Holy Trinity, the Guildhall, Whitefriargate –
Dropping leaflets?
Toddle off, my songs; go to the lutes
Of untuned strings, played by God's mutes,

And make no mark, subside with no pock
Or ripple in the sane mud. More dirt, more dirt!
In the botched fog of outcries, the political sandwiches –
The sky is high, and so am I –
Ah, they say, the same neat suit and tidy ties.

Restraint

It lives in the body,
Interior clothing
Woven under nakedness

On constant looms. Textile
Animal, it feeds on words,
Evasions that trick

What might have been
To what was never tried.
It laughs its head off

At funerals, is safe
And satisfied, the only
Creature ever satisfied.

A long course in freedom
Hurts it. It cries out
And makes you tell lies.

The Disguise

A funeral procession of barges
On industrial canals –
The nineteenth century, and last,
Celebrating itself, through counties
Ditched and bricked with its epitaphs.

History is illiterate.
It is 'effects', wars, 'conditions',
Boots at dawn and the closing of doors,
Ambition at its conferences.
Most live in an aftermath of its injustices.

And they say, 'Go out smiling, let your poems
Tickle the ribs of Optimism
On an absolute prosody that ticks over
With the strength of an intricate machine,
Not this free verse you can buy at Woolworths.'

But I *am* smiling, and against you.
There is an invective of grins, winks, fingers,
Up the sleeves of galactic offspring.
Through your trash go their impertinent smiles,
Hidden by glum masks, the finest insult.

from Barbarians

'He was bored, but nevertheless he slowly grew further and further away from the hardship and simplicity of the workers, from his childhood environment. He somehow learned how to behave, as they say. Without realizing it, he cut himself off from his own people. . . . He thought he was merely bored, but secretly he was flattered at being included. Some forces drew him towards the bourgeoisie; other forces sought to retard his transition.'

'The truth of life was on the side of the men who returned to their poor houses, on the side of the men who had not "made good".'

Paul Nizan, *Antoine Bloyé*

The Come-on

'. . . the guardian, the king's son, who kept watch over the gates
of the garden in which I wanted to live.'
                                    Albert Camus

To have watched the soul of my people
    Fingered by the callous
Enlivens the bitter ooze from my grudge.
    Mere seepage from 'background'
Takes over, blacking out what intellect
    Was nursed by school or book
Or had accrued by questioning the world.
    Enchanting, beloved texts
Searched in for a generous mandate for
    Believing who I am,
What I have lived and felt, might just as well
    Not exist when the vile
Come on with their 'coals in the bath' stories
    Or mock at your accent.
Even now I am an embarrassment
    To myself, my candour.
Listen now to the 'professional classes'
    Renewing claims to 'rights',
Possession of land, ownership of work,
    Decency of 'standards'.
In the bleep-bleep of versicles, leisure-novels,
    Black traffic of Oxbridge –
Books and bicycles, the bile of success –
    Men dressed in prunella
Utter credentials and their culture rules us,
    A culture of connivance,
Of 'authority', arts of bland recoveries.
    Where, then, is 'poetry'?

[99]

Brothers, they say that we have no culture.
    We are of the wrong world,
Our level is the popular, the media,
    The sensational columns,
Unless we enter through a narrow gate
    In a wall they have built
To join them in the 'disinterested tradition'
    Of tea, of couplets dipped
In sherry and the decanted, portentous remark.
    Therefore, we'll deafen them
With the dull staccato of our typewriters.
    But do not misbehave –
Threats and thrashings won't work: we're outnumbered.
    Drink ale if you must still,
But learn to tell one good wine from another –
    Our honesty is cunning.
We will beat them with decorum, with manners,
    As sly as language is.
Take tea with the king's son at the seminars –
    He won't know what's happening.
Carry your learning as does the mimic his face.
    Know one knife from another.
You will lose heart: don't show it. Be patient;
    And sit on that high wall
In its obstacle glass chips, its barbed wire,
    Watching the gardeners.
One day we will leap down, into the garden,
    And open the gate – *wide, wide.*
We too shall be kings' sons and guardians,
    And then there will be no wall:
Our grudges will look quaint and terrible.

In the Grounds

Yorkshire, 1975

Barbarians in a garden, softness does
Approve of who we are as it does those
Who when we speak proclaim us barbarous
And say we have no business with the rose.

Gently the grass waves, and its green applauds
The justice, not of progress, but of growth.
We walk as people on the paths of gods
And in our minds we harmonize them both.

Disclosures of these grounds – a river view,
Two Irish wolfhounds watching on a lawn;
A spinster with her sewing stares at you,
And begs you leave her pretty world alone.

More books than prejudice in our young minds . . .
We could not harm her, would not, would prefer
A noise less military and more kind
Than our boots make across her wide *parterre*.

We are intransigent, at odds with them.
They see our rabble-dreams as new contempt
For England's art of house and leaf. Condemn
Our clumsiness – you do not know, how, unkempt

And coarse, we hurt a truth with truth, still true
To who we are: barbarians, whose chins
Drool with ale-stinking hair, whose horses chew
Turf owned by watching, frightened mandarins,

Their surly nephews lounging at each gate,
Afraid we'll steal their family's treasured things,
Then hawk them – pictures, furniture and plate –
Round the encampments of our saddle-kings.

Here be Dragons
Pomponius Mela, Chorographia

In Africa, Pomponius Mela wrote,
Are tribes whose bodies stop below the throat.
His readers might not marvel much at that
Headless and monstrous proletariat
For Mela says that faces on their chests
Had all the usual features and, unless
Pomponius lied, I can suppose their art,
Doubtless oral, came straight from the heart.

There, too, in Africa, were troglodytes
Who housed themselves in the eternal night.
This Mela proffers civilized distaste.
He says of these non-citizens of waste
And downward-tunnelled tenements, they dined
On serpents they discovered as they mined.
But had they raised their tenements through sky,
What lunch would fowl-fed Mela specify?

Mela records a tribe that cursed the sun
At dusk and dawn. These people of No-One
Possessed no names and did not dream. Dreamless
Without nomenclature, did Mela bless
That dreamless people who knew more than he
Could ever know of their reality,
Cursing the sun, cursing at dusk and dawn,
For reasons Romans couldn't lay their fingers on?

These then were wonders Mela thought he saw
In lives reported as hair, skin and claw.
That flattered Rome, to keep its *regnum* sure –
The home of shave and soap and manicure.
One story's left, the one that Mela tells
That's their revenge – the one about the well.
Arriving there, thirsty and out of breath,
Romans might drink, then laugh themselves to death.

Gardeners

England, Loamshire, 1789
A gardener speaks, in the grounds of a great house,
to his Lordship

Gardens, gardens, and we are gardeners . . .
Razored hedgerow, flowers, those planted trees
Whose avenues conduct a greater ease
Of shadow to your own and ladies' skins
And tilt this Nature to magnificence
And natural delight. But pardon us,
My Lord, if we reluctantly admit
Our horticulture not the whole of it,
Forgetting, that for you, this elegance
Is not our work, but your far tidier Sense.

Out of humiliation comes that sweet
Humility that does no good. We know
Our coarser artistries will make things grow.
Others design the craftsmanship we fashion
To please your topographical possession.
A small humiliation – Yes, we eat,
Our crops and passions tucked out of the view
Across a shire, the name of which is you,
Where every native creature runs upon
Hills, moors and meadows which your named eyes own.

Our eyes are nameless, generally turned
Towards the earth our fingers sift all day –
Your day, your earth, your eyes, wearing away
Not earth, eyes, days, but scouring, forcing down
What lives in us and which you cannot own.
One of us heard the earth cry out. It spurned
His hands. It threw stones in his face. We found
That man, my Lord, and he was mad. We bound
His hands together and we heard him say –
'Not me! Not me who cries!' We took away

That man – remember, Lord? – and then we turned,
Hearing your steward order us return,
His oaths, and how you treated us with scorn.
They call this grudge. Let me hear you admit
That in the country that's but half of it.
Townsmen will wonder, when your house was burned,
We did not burn your gardens and undo
What likes of us did for the likes of you;
We did not raze this garden that we made,
Although we hanged you somewhere in its shade.

The Student
Of Renfrewshire, 1820

For our Mechanics' Literary Club
I study Tacitus. It takes all night
At this rough country table which I scrub
Before I sit at it, by candlelight,
Spreading my books on it. I think respect
Must work like love in any intellect.
    Difficult Latin sticks in my throat
    And the scarecrow wears my coat.

What put me up to it, this partnership
Of lexicon and text, these five books thieved,
These two books borrowed, handed down, this grip
Of mind on mind, this work? Am I deceived?
Is literature a life proved much too good
To have its place in our coarse neighbourhood?
    Difficult Latin sticks in my throat
    And the scarecrow wears my coat.

In Paisley when they read the Riot Act
We faced the horsemen of the 10th Hussars.
Men's bones were broken, angry heads were cracked –
Provosts, sheriffs, guns and iron bars.
We thrashed the poet William Motherwell,
That depute-sheriff and the law's law-minstrel.
    Difficult Latin sticks in my throat
    And the scarecrow wears my coat.

Between us and our lives were bayonets.
They shone like water. We were crooked with thirst,
That hot dry bubbling when your whole life sweats.
'If you want life', they said, 'you must die first.'
Thus in a drought of fear Republic died
On Linen Street, Lawn Street and Causeyside.
    Difficult Latin sticks in my throat
    And the scarecrow wears my coat.

Beneath our banners I was marching for
My scholarship of barley, secret work
On which authority must slam its door
As Rome on Goth, Byzantium on Turk.
I'm left to guess their books, which precious line,
Eluding me, is never to be mine.
    Difficult Latin sticks in my throat
    And the scarecrow wears my coat.

Frost, poverty, rare, rare, the rapid rain . . .
What good can come of study, I must have.
I read it once, then read it twice again.
Fox, whittrick, dog, my horse, my new-born calf –
Let me recite my life, my animals and clay,
My candlelight, my fuddled melody.
    Difficult Latin sticks in my throat
    And the scarecrow wears my coat.

Such hard work urges me to turn each line
As firmly as I plough a furrow straight,
By doing so make this work clandestine,
Mix its affections with both love and hate.
So, Tacitus, old friend, though not to me,
Allow me master your authority.
    Difficult Latin sticks in my throat
    And the scarecrow wears my coat.

Empires

All the dead Imperia . . . They have gone
Taking their atlases and grand pianos.
They could not leave geography alone.
They conquered with the thistle and the rose.
To our forefathers it was right to raise
Their pretty flag at every foreign dawn
Then lower it at sunset in a haze
Of bugle-brass. They interfered with place,
Time, people, lives, and so to bed. They died
When it died. It had died before. It died
Before they did. They did not know it. Race,
Power, Trade, Fleet, a hundred regiments,
Postponed that final reckoning with pride,
Which was expensive. Counting up the cost
We plunder morals from the power they lost.
They ruined us. They conquered continents.
We filled their uniforms. We cruised the seas.
We worked their mines and made their histories.
You work, we rule, they said. We worked; they ruled.
They fooled the tenements. All men were fooled.
It still persists. It will be so, always.
Listen. An out-of-work apprentice plays
God Save the Queen on an Edwardian flute.
He is, but does not know it, destitute.

The Wealth

When he returned to New York in December 1965, he figured his stay would be a brief one, that he'd earn $25,000 if he was lucky, enough to live comfortably in England. Instead, he earned ten times that much. The success – and the terrors that accompanied it – had begun.

Paul Cowan, on Paul Simon
Rolling Stone, 1 July, 1976

If I prove nothing to you, it's my fault.
The planet's round and greedy.
This song-infatuated globe can't handle it,
In love with rip-off and reward.

It is an old perdition to be rich,
An old displeasure to be seen dismayed
With what you wanted, when, having it, it hurts
Or turns against you in the night.

The last day of December '65
I got a letter from your Uncle Sam.
I'd thought of him as one of the good guys,
Stern, dressed in a dollar, but on our side.

By then I was in two minds.
A lot of people were dying, like clichés.
I wasn't even an American.
Gabe read my papers over, then we hit the town.

The Go-Go girls brought New Year in
Dancing on our table – *Sloopy, hang on!*
I didn't lose my mind in drink. I sulked.
The night-club scooped me up and took me home.

I walked to the bus depot in the snow.
January. They took us to Cleveland.
I didn't want to go. Nick said, 'Go. Buy time.'
We walked around, afraid in underpants.

Faced with a form, I opted for the Coastguard,
'And don't let me see any damn fool
Write "coastguard", gentlemen,' yelled a sailor.
There were six-foot-six football giants

Who fainted away in the lottery
Of the blood-test. I wouldn't have missed it,
Not for anything. I didn't faint. I felt –
I felt *proud*. And then *I* couldn't pee in the cup.

A doctor said, if he was me, he'd go back
To Scotland. 'Randall Jarrell,' I said.
The man next in line pushed me, and asked
If I was 'some kinda coward'. 'Yes,' I said.

I said I wasn't an American.
You can't say that to a man in blue jockey-shorts
Who'd been insisting on the Marine Corps.
'A medical is close enough,' I said.

If that man went to Vietnam, I hope
He didn't die, or kill anyone,
Or help reduce thin children to
An orphanage of ash.

We used to visit in Peninsula, Ohio,
A precious farmhouse on a wooded hill.
I planted corn, walked on an Indian trail,
James Fenimore Cooper for a day.

The poems in my head were facing west
Towards a continental summer.
I won't deny it. The Stars and Stripes
On a blue autumn day is quite something.

But then, so was I, in casuals,
Fit and young, athletic, frivolous –
As if nobody knew me then – one round year married,
My wife in tears at having to go home so soon.

I liked old villages with soldier-statued squares
Where I could stand and feel like Robert Lowell.
Still there, and probably the same,
Each with its radical son and its casualty.

States of long trains and the astounding autumn,
I squeaked before your laws, reduced
To nakedness, my penis in a cup
Refusing Uncle Sam his specimen of me –

My health, portrayed in Akron's
Tax-paid chemicals, *Cutty Sark*,
Upper New York State wine – oh, Liz, *your* wine! –
And food bought in the Kroger Store.

We shipped aboard SS *United States*.
I went home on a name
With nothing like enough
To live on comfortably.

I felt like a Jew, at Hamburg
On a boat bound for America,
A Jew at Hamburg, 1939,
And wept for laws, but not for me, civilian,

Writing poetry, seasick on the North Atlantic,
Reading *Henderson the Rain King*
And *For the Union Dead*.
I wanted it torpedoed, by the British.

But, for you, a terror was beginning . . .
Such is the magnitude of song.
An American critic, writing of
An English poet who thinks himself classical,

Has said of tenderness, it is
'The social face of self-pity'.
If I say, tenderly, I am afraid,
Who do I fear, or what? *Horror*. 'The wealth! The wealth!'

America, I admit it. You've beaten me.
I'll end up in a regiment of *foederati*
To be led forever by a minor Belisarius
Against my kin in the forests of Europe.

Our armoured herds are grazing on the map.
And so are theirs. I write this for *détente*,
Which, as ever, should be personal.
One false move then, I'd have no right to speak.

In your culture, I am a barbarian,
But I'm that here, and everywhere,
Lulled by alien rites, lullabyed with remorse
Here on the backstreets of the universe.

Elegy for the Lost Parish

Dream, ploughman, of what agriculture brings,
Your eggs, your bacon to your greasy plate;
Then listen to the evening's thrush that sings
Exhilarated sadness and the intimate.

Your son's in Canada, growing his wheat
On fields the size of farms, and prosperous
On grain and granary. His world's replete
With life and love and house and happiness.

Dream, ploughman, of the lovely girl who died
So many summers gone, whose face will come
To you, call to you, and be deified
In sunlight on one cut chrysanthemum.

A nod of nettles flutters its green dust
Across small fields where you have mown the hay.
So wipe your brow, as on a scented gust
Your past flies in and will not go away.

Dream, ploughman, of old characters you've known
Who taught you things of scythe and horse and plough;
Of fields prepared, seed rhythmically sown,
Their ways of work that are forgotten now.

Remember, sir, and let them come to you
Out of your eye to mutter requiem,
Praising fidelities, the good of you.
Allow their consolations, cherish them

Into a privacy, as, with hand's slow shake
You reach towards your glass, your hands reach to
Where no one is or can be. Heartbreak,
Heartbreak and loneliness of virtue!

Watches of Grandfathers

They go with corporations
And with fountain pens,
With honour and inscription,
Fastidious longevities
In which are reckoned
The funerals of friends.

Worn in relation to work,
Timetables, opening times,
And counterparts carried by
Despicable referees,
They are neat in the palm of a hand.
Always to be dangled before

Babies in prams, consulted
With flourishes that invite
Benevolent side-glances,
They have a kindness
Which the artistry of time
In its steady circles

Denies, as it measures
Proximity to pensionable age,
Or, from a safe hook
In the corner of a workshop,
Hung there, stare at the bench
As they mutter 'Death, Death'.

They long for the pocket
Of the eldest son, in
The waistcoat he will buy for one,
Who will see his father's eye
Glazed on it, and the age
Of his sons slowly numbered.

Portrait Photograph, 1915

We too have our place, who were not photographed
So much and then only in multitudes
Rising from holes in the ground to fall into smoke
Or is it newsreel beyond newsreel
But I do not know and I have lost my name
And my face and as for dignity
I never had it in any case, except once,
I think, in the High Street, before we left
For troopships and the farewell pipers,
When it was my turn in the queue
In Anderson's Photographic Arcade and Salon,
In my uniform, and I was not a tall man
Although for a moment I had a sense
Of posterity in the eyes of descendants,
Of my own face in a frame on a small table
Over which her eyes would go, and my sons',
And that I would persist, in day and night,
Fading a little as they say they do.

The Musician

They've told me MacAuley is gone now
Taking his tool-box and both his fiddles.
They are saying, *'What will we do now?*
There is no music in this or the next parish.'

Until a replacement is found there
Not one note will be heard after whist
Unless it is played from a record –
That, even the young say, won't be as good.

They will talk of MacAuley for ever there,
Long after their own receipt of pensions,
Of his carpenter's wrist on the fiddle-bow
Stitching like mad through jig-time.

And so I have heard on the telephone
MacAuley is gone now, and both his fiddles
Lie in their cases under the stairs
With the music we never knew he could read.

It is Beethoven and Bach, they tell me,
And a very fat volume, a German tutor,
That cost six shillings before the war,
And its pages, they tell me, are black with notes.

It's your carpenter's wrist they remember
In love with your local tradition.
Your carpenter's fist could not break through
To the public of Bach and Beethoven.

So they've told me MacAuley is gone,
Both his fiddles lie under the stairs now
With music by Bach and Beethoven
Beside six bob's worth of ambition.

Let them open your window frames, open your doors,
Think, as they sit on their mended chairs,
Of you, their musician, and doctor to wood,
That no one has heard what you understood.

Drowning

Why give the place its name, when it has changed,
Where, in the grasping waters of the Gryfe,
He, his name forgotten now, was drowned?
What is remembered is his little life.

Ask any man of forty-odd or so,
He'd think a bit, as if he had to try
To bring that name back from its tragedy,
Though, struggling with the tide, he saw him die.

One I could ask was wild, swam in the buff
Where Gryfe's clean waters raced the greedy Clyde
Beside that bridge where ladies parked and watched.
To dry himself, he ran the countryside.

Kirk elder now, who shot the sparrows down
With airgun resting on a garden fence,
How fares your soul, handing out the hymnals,
Who in your sin worked wicked innocence?

One I could ask has crossed the Scottish seas.
From Canada, we've heard no news at all.
He took his boots, his two sly winger's feet.
We miss that man as if he'd pinched our ball.

Most stayed at home, or near it, so they drink
On Friday nights or Saturdays and where
Men know each other and suppress remarks
On sagging bellies or receding hair.

One I could ask has fired his life away
With bottle after bottle to his mouth,
Raw liquor in the turpitude of ditches
While blubbering a sermon on his youth.

Ask any man of forty-odd or so
Around that parish by the Clyde's run sweat,
He'll shake his head as if he has forgotten,
Then walk away, and wish he could forget.

Remember, how we ran up to the bank
And, naked, how we screamed and jumped right in?
Those ladies, watching, must have thought we tried
To please them with a courtesy of skin.

That was our time, and after he was drowned.
It did not mean we had forgotten him.
It is a law, to disobey scared parents.
What better pool than his in which to swim?

But watch the changing waters, when the tide
Runs up, its shoulders hunched, with winking eyes,
And with a nip of sea and a dark surface
It steals the calm reflection from the sky.

They worked him free. They packed his clothes around
   him.
They sat him on his bike and wheeled him home.
Too young for swimming then, I was in goal,
When, from our pitch, I saw the dead boys come.

Glasgow Schoolboys, Running Backwards

High wind . . . They turn their backs to it, and push.
Their crazy strides are chopped in little steps.
And all their lives, like that, they'll have to rush
Forwards in reverse, always holding their caps.

Red Buses

'The last Western'

Galoot and lover, homeward drunks
Through Govan, Linthouse, Renfrew Cross
Have known well the sudden lurch
Of double-deckers to the digestive system.
God help the man who pukes on his seat
Or is tempted to impertinence.
He will have no Requiem.
Nor in the Golf Inn will there be sung
Delicate character studies;
No pawky *éloge* in the Wallace Arms
Nor in the crowds of Glasgow be missed
Among umbrellas and young women in
Greatcoats selling *Morning Star*.
For these are the plain facts of the matter:
No longer will singing be tolerated
Nor the mess created by those
Who cannot hold it in, but who
Must for ever be incontinent.
From now on are conductresses instructed
To put the boot in at the first signs of
Contraventions of these Orders –
And our women, as you know, are worse than our men,
Whose only function is,
In this business, to take prisoners.
Therefore, you who have lost your hearts
In San Francisco or who sing
Of your mother's eyes, take warning . . .
Already you will have heard how
Sundry gung-ho Yankee submariners
Have found themselves airborne at Bishopton.
They walked around, amazed

[124]

In the night of council houses.
One we heard of slept in the garden
Of a distinguished JP, waking
Under a coverlet of leaves and dew
To sing sad songs of Ohio
Or wherever it was he came from.
We will no longer brook misbehaviour,
Not even from presbyterians.
So, revise your youths. Forget
Your indiscretions on the back-seat
And the disasters of carry-outs
In paper-bags not strong enough
For the purpose. From now on you will walk home.
If it drives you crazy to listen to
Softly ticking factories; or if
Under the tenements you feel you are
In a Glencoe of the mind; or if
Cranes, shipyards, sleeping it off
In the sweat of forgotten labour
Are better served in peace than you are;
Or if, by the bonded warehouses,
You see the square root of all distillations;
Or if you have forgotten the road
And get lost for ever in the first
Mattress of West-bracken, the first
Gaunt countryside of the West, then that
Is your fault. You will not be alone.

Ballad of the Two Left Hands

When walking out one morning
  Walking down Clydeside Street
I met a man with two left hands
  Who said he was obsolete.

At noon the work horns sounded through
  The shipyards on Clyde's shore
And told men that the day had come
  When they'd work there no more.

Economy is hand and sweat
  A welder in his mask
A new apprentice pouring tea
  From his father's thermos flask.

And soon these men of several trades
  Stood there on Clydeside Street
Stood staring at each new left hand
  That made them obsolete.

'Beware of men in suits,' one said
  'Take it from me, it's true
Their drivel economics'll
  Put two left hands on you.'

All in the afternoon was shut
  When I walked out again
The day had pulled on its black gloves
  And turned its back on men.

I walked the dusk of darkened cranes
  Clyde broke on Clyde's dark shore
And rivets fired where men still work
  Though men work here no more.

High in the night's dark universe
  I saw the promised star
That men I knew raise glasses to
  In an illegal bar.

They toast that city still to come
  Where truth and justice meet
And though they don't know where it is
  It's not on Clydeside Street.

With thumbs stuck on the wrong way round
  In two left-footed shoes
I saw a man search in his heart
  And ask it, 'Are you true?'

That man who sat on Clydeside Street
  Looked up at me and said
'I'll study this, then I'll pick clean
  The insides of my head.'

And moonlight washed the shipyards then
  Each crane was hung with stars
Rinsed in the moonlight we stared up
  Like old astronomers.

Economy is hand and sweat
  And foundrymen and fire
Revise your textbooks, multiply
  Your guilt by your desire.

Such dignity, so many lives,
    Even on Clydeside Street
When mind and heart together ask
    'Why are we obsolete?'

Lost Gloves

I leave my body in a new blue suit
  With my soul, which is newly destitute.
Rinsed spirit of me, washed for this departure,
  Takes off adroitly to its atmosphere.

And here's that blue glove on a railing's tip
  Where iron, frost and wool make partnership
Of animal and elements and blue –
  Lost little glove, I still remember you.

You do not fit my hand now, nor can I fit
  My world with life; nor my mouth match its spit;
My tongue, my words; my eyes, the things they see.
  My head is upside down in memory.

A child walks to his mother, right hand bare
  And hidden in his coat, then follows her
Inside, his gloved hand on the banister,
  His right hand on his heart, remaining there.

My pulse beats backwards to a street in winter –
  Blue first perceived, that I now disinter
Blue out of blue where life and childhood crossed:
  Five blue wool-fingers waving in the frost.

Stories

Once, once, O once upon a time –
I wish that's how a poem could begin,
And so begin one. That's how stories should.
The sweet parental voices started so,
Opening a book, *my* book, one given by
An aunt and uncle, inscribed 'for Christmas'.

No story ever did, I think, unless
Its author, sitting down, said, 'O I wish
That *this* is how a story could begin,'
And so began, his tongue half in his cheek.
Once, once, O once upon a time –
It's real, magnanimous, and true! I wish,

And wish, and so my friends lose patience with
My stories and they say, 'So this piece is
A story of lost gloves, and, yes, I know
I lost *my* gloves, but why this story, *this*,
This *making-up*?' *Once, once, O once upon
A time*, before gloves, gauntlets, politics . . .

Never, never, never, never, never . . .
That's a *good* line. And there was one which took
My senses to adventure on a day
Of wind and rain . . . 'One more step, Mr Hands,
And I'll blow your brains out!' *Once, once, once, once* . . .
I think the alphabet is tired of life.

'But be contemporary!' they shout, thumping
The table, and 'Yes, Yes,' I say, 'I'll buy
That, all or nothing. Just you wait, you'll see.
I'm of the times . . . My pulse is topical,
And I love all the things I'm meant to love,
Am civil and "sincere", one of the boys.'

Ah, that's better. I mean, I mean it *all*.
Yet when I start to write, my pen puts down
Once, once, O once upon a time . . .
And that's for nothing and for no one,
Not anyone, not even for a child
Who, at a table by a bowl of fruit,

Sits down to read. It is too personal,
One sorry pass. I'll give away my thought
Of knowing that a life-discarded petal
Fell down, so slowly, when, a child, I read,
And landed on a page and was brushed off.
Once, once, O once, that happened so, like that –

Tender descent – and for a moment was
Completed by its image on the polished
Table. I took it in, did not forget.
Then, *am* I good? Was *that* benevolent?
Now, dignity of tables and of books,
What do *you* say? *'There is no answer, friend.'*

Stranger's Grief

i.m. Robert Lowell

It's as if I've grown old, sitting like this
In a small park by the Lot in Cahors
Where autumn is arriving through its mist
To surprise my life with its metaphor.

In an *Observer*, four days out of date,
I've read the poet Lowell's dead. . . . New York,
New York, where smoke and whisky concentrate
Their traffic, architecture, art and work.

Across this river which is brown and fast
There is a paddock boys are running round,
Each one determined not to finish last.
Breath from their mouths drags after them like sound.

That's where the summer stops and autumn starts.
A gentle cadence in the wind will sing
Natural elegies, its counterparts
Of human sadness drowned in everything.

Youth's country is impossibly across
A wide river. How anyone can come
From there, and not look back, or feel no loss,
Always amazes me. I call youth *home*;

I'd go back if I could. I don't feel warmed
By death. To die is nothing very grand.
This world is delicate and misinformed.
It's growing old I've failed to understand.

What else can I do, feeling this way, but sit
With my wife and my newspaper, well-fed,
Well-wined, happy together and unfit.
Is it a happiness like this, being dead?

A radio, its non-specific song
Far away in a leafy park . . . I'm full
Of my routine sadness. It can't be wrong
To let these thoughts run free and overrule

Tranquillity, absorbing time and place,
And what I've read, and you and me, each half
Of this one silent couple, face to face,
As still as lovers in a lithograph.

It is like waiting, learning how to die,
Opened to sweetness, neutral as a leaf
Watching leaves falling. Notice how they lie,
How each survivor shares each stranger's grief.

Night-Devon, Dawn-Devon

It is with fear, with shame also we raise
Embarrassed eyes to placid galaxies
Where science, stars and planets graze
In fields of God-knows-what. Impieties,
Michael, impieties, that flatter nerve
As does this morning dew on naked feet,
A relish of something. We do deserve
Better than this, our metres obsolete
Contraptions with which words might seize
Wingbeat of kingfisher, the breeze
Through which it flew, or a berry that glows
So close upon a girl's cheek they are the same
And metaphors. We take the blame. It goes.
It leaves us faceless, two smiles in a frame.

On Her Picture Left with Him

On trains to London and the south
  And thus away from me
These words in my enamoured mouth
  Summon the flattery
Of who it is and what I love,
  Distracting me.

Lady, so far outside, and gone,
  Your picture left with me
Is like the world I look upon
  And shows reality
As who it is and why I love,
  Distracting me.

Thus do I gaze on you, and drink
  Your face you left with me,
And speak to you in whispered ink
  With that humility
Which is a lesser spoil of love,
  Distracting me.

Now is the afternoon turned round
  To dusk that darkens me,
And walking on nocturnal ground
  Offers no liberty
From who I am and who I love,
  Distracting me.

Old Things

Time and removal vans
Scatter dead widows
From their dying children.
It is late, secretly.
It is a late era
In the grey-stilted rain.
And you who pilfer
In shops of second-hand
Among shabby heirlooms,
Accumulating bits
Of blue pottery, a chair,
A vase, a baby-grand,
Consider – now it's late –
What things come up for air
Out of such furniture,
Whose-hands in the polish,
What-lover's-eye upon
Pendants of amethyst,
Whose-name you wear inside
Whose-bangle on your wrist.

Wedding

Confetti in the gutters,
Half a dozen leaves
That reach here from autumn,
Yearly . . . What point is there
In regretting no shrubbery
Or abundance of green
Hallows this couple, when the car
The groom has worked on for weeks
Takes them down a street
Elated by love and community?
There is one season
For poverty, and delight
Overlaps all things.

The Return

'Grey skies are just clouds passing over.'
Duke Ellington

The window-cleaner carried
A cloth bag full of change
And it rattled the tariff
Of window-panes.

There are his ladders
Left by the wall.
There is his pail. There is his rag.
But the windows are broken.

Houses are empty
And rusting aerials sing
A congress of metal and wind
And indifferent sparrows.

Gushed soot on the hearths,
Heaps of plaster, split timbers,
Sodden newsprint and wreckage of armchairs
Litter ripped living-rooms.

I dreamt of perfection.
My dreams have come home
To die here and cling to
My anarchy of convictions.

If only there were no such troubles.
My politics vanished
To the end of the street
Where beauty and pollution meet

In natural ecstasy,
A hint of trees
By the abandoned railway
And a red sunset.

And this is the house I owned,
My two sufficient rooms.
There is no trace of me
As I look for signs

Of 'little jobs' I did about the house,
Domestic, studious, and in love,
Three things, or so I'm told,
I should have fought against.

from St Kilda's Parliament

St Kilda's Parliament: 1879–1979

The photographer revisits his picture

On either side of a rock-paved lane,
Two files of men are standing barefooted,
Bearded, waistcoated, each with a tam-o'-shanter
On his head, and most with a set half-smile
That comes from their companionship with rock,
With soft mists, with rain, with roaring gales,
And from a diet of solan goose and eggs,
A diet of dulse and sloke and sea-tangle,
And ignorance of what a pig, a bee, a rat,
Or rabbit look like, although they remember
The three apples brought here by a traveller
Five years ago, and have discussed them since.
And there are several dogs doing nothing
Who seem contemptuous of my camera,
And a woman who might not believe it
If she were told of the populous mainland.
A man sits on a bank by the door of his house,
Staring out to sea and at a small craft
Bobbing there, the little boat that brought me here,
Whose carpentry was slowly shaped by waves,
By a history of these northern waters.
Wise men or simpletons – it is hard to tell –
But in that way they almost look alike
You also see how each is individual,
Proud of his shyness and of his small life
On this outcast of the Hebrides
With his eyes full of weather and seabirds,
Fish, and whatever morsel he grows here.
Clear, too, is manhood, and how each man looks
Secure in the love of a woman who
Also knows the wisdom of the sun rising,

Of weather in the eyes like landmarks.
Fifty years before depopulation –
Before the boats came at their own request
To ease them from their dying babies –
It was easy, even then, to imagine
St Kilda return to its naked self,
Its archaeology of hazelraw
And footprints stratified beneath the lichen.
See, how simple it all is, these toes
Playfully clutching the edge of a boulder.
It is a remote democracy, where men,
In manacles of place, outstare a sea
That rattes back its manacles of salt,
The moody jailer of the wild Atlantic.
           Traveller, tourist with your mind set on
Romantic Staffas and materials for
Winter conversations, if you should go there,
Landing at sunrise on its difficult shores,
On St Kilda you will surely hear Gaelic
Spoken softly like a poetry of ghosts
By those who never were contorted by
Hierarchies of cuisine and literacy.
You need only look at the faces of these men
Standing there like everybody's ancestors,
This flick of time I shuttered on a face.
Look at their sly, assuring mockery.
They are aware of what we are up to
With our internal explorations, our
Designs of affluence and education.
They know us so well, and are not jealous,
Whose be-all and end-all was an eternal
Casual husbandry upon a toehold
Of Europe, which, when failing, was not their fault.
You can see they have already prophesied
A day when survivors look across the stern

[144]

Of a departing vessel for the last time
At their gannet-shrouded cliffs, and the farewells
Of the St Kilda mouse and St Kilda wren
As they fall into the texts of specialists,
Ornithological visitors at the prow
Of a sullenly managed boat from the future.
They pose for ever outside their parliament,
Looking at me, as if they have grown from
Affection scattered across my own eyes.
And it is because of this that I, who took
This photograph in a year of many events –
The Zulu massacres, Tchaikovsky's opera –
Return to tell you this, and that after
My many photographs of distressed cities,
My portraits of successive elegants,
Of the emaciated dead, the lost empires,
Exploded fleets, and of the writhing flesh
Of dead civilians and commercial copulations,
That after so much of that larger franchise
It is to this island that I return.
Here I whittle time, like a dry stick,
From sunrise to sunset, among the groans
And sighings of a tongue I cannot speak,
Outside a parliament, looking at them,
As they, too, must always look at me
Looking through my apparatus at them
Looking. Benevolent, or malign? But who,
At this late stage, could tell, or think it worth it?
For I was there, and am, and I forget.

The Apple Tree

'And if the world should end tomorrow,
I still would plant my apple tree.'
                                    Luther

I could play the bad eras like a concertina.
Multiple chords would squeak like 'Excuse me',
'I beg your pardon', 'Oops' and 'Sorry, no thank you.'
Pump hard on a squeeze-box and you can almost hear
The Protestant clerks of northern Europe in Hell,
Complaisant men who filed the paperwork of death
Or signed the warrants, exemplary in private life
But puritanical before their desks of duty.
Say what you like, their Gods did not approve of them.

Men moaned of Scotland that its barren air and soil
Couldn't so much as ripen an apple. I can hear
Their croaked whispers reproach the stern and wild of
   Alba,
Naming our Kirk, our character, our coarse consent
To drunken decency and sober violence,
Our paradox of ways. Here, in the lovely land,
Beside Kirkmaiden, enumerating apple trees,
I feel the simple millions groan, 'Keep you your faith.
A sapling nursed to fruit impersonates salvation.'

Kirk-sanctioned crimes, Kirk-flourished trade, Kirk-coded
  commerce –
Say what you like, our Gods have not approved of them
While apples ripen round the mist-mild farms and
  gardens.
Good nature and a scent of fruit at dailygone
Make more of our acceptances and affirmations
Than quick links forced from character to climate.
Name you our beasts and trees, our rivers raced with fish,
Our islands, oceans, mountains and our field-sweet crops.
These too define a people named in city stone.

Four horses chew among the windfalls. Fallen fruits
Spill sweetening juices on the orchard grass, frosted
Into their leaking bruises and hoofed into pulp.
Last wasps grow fat and a tantrum of stings threatens
The man on his ladder, who cups an apple in
The stretch of his hand, then plucks it down, to bite
Its greeny red, rubbed on his overalls. He stands
Up there, eating an apple among all the apples
While big mares and their foals munch on the apple-grass.

At night the orchard is a brew of leaf and fruit,
Feeling the pinch of autumn. Spread sneddins release
The sounds that lie in wait in wood, and over there
An upland wilderness reposes in chilled beauty.
Burns spate with cleanliness of rain, that clean high
  ground
Carrion crow and left-alone mountain sheep administer.
Crag-country, wet and wiry, but fertile to the eye;
A lung-and-heart testing land, but by a ruin there
You will find crab-apple trees, black harp-strings in the
  wind.

Tonight I saw the stars trapped underneath the water.
I signed the simple covenant we keep with love.
One hand held out an apple while the other held
Earth from a kirkyard where the dead remember me.
In these lost hollows of the stern conventicles
A faith is kept with land and fruit. Already are
New scriptures written by the late-arriving autumn,
That postponed shuffle of leaves, that white frost-writing.
These are my missionary fruits, a kindred taste.

Then let my Gods be miracles brought on stone boats
By Conval and the first dailyday folk before him.
Rather an ordinary joy – a girl with a basket,
With apples under a linen cloth – than comfortless
With windlestrae to eat. Forge no false links of man
To land or creed, the true are good enough. Our lives
Crave codes of courtesy, ways of describing love,
And these, in a good-natured land, are ways to weep,
True comfort as you wipe your eyes and try to live.

An Address on the Destitution of Scotland

Who would have thought it, and not me, not me,
That a boy who shawed turnips with a large gully
By the side of Cousar's cart and snort-breathed
   Clydesdale,
Who worked in the blue-and-red darkening dusk of
   childhood,
Would grow into this archivist of Red desires?
Far away are the chills of original Octobers.
My eyes are heavy now with alien perspectives,
And I am sick of the decisions of philosophers –
Dirty hands, dirty hands of turncoats and opinion-makers.
It was a long road back to this undeclared Republic.
I came by the by-ways, empty of milestones,
On the roads of old drovers, by disused workings.

So here I am, returned to your shabby encampments.
I, too, have scrounged on open fields, ripped up
Into their gathering of released good stinks
That mingle in the first-few-hours-of-shaws-rotting,
That reek of roots, that tactile, lunatic aroma
Tasting of dialect and curses sent out to work.
Tell me of your tinkerdom, of this poverty
Among you, raddled by a destitute polity,
The fields abandoned to old supermarket trolleys,
An ancient soot, the Clyde returning to its nature.
On which blasphemy do you blame your outcast silence,
Bedraggled here with your billy-cans and supper?

Share with me, then, the sad glugs in your bottles;
Throw a stolen spud for me on the side-embers.
Allow me to pull up a brick, and to sit beside you
In this nocturne of modernity, to speak of the dead,
Of the creatures loping from their dens of extinction.
Who are you waiting for? The stern mountain-preacher
In his coat of biblical night? I have seen him.
He sleeps in a kiln, out of the way of dragoons;
And I met a subversive optimist, at Sanquhar.
Permit me, then, to join your circle around your fire
In this midden of warm faces and freezing backs.
Sing me your songs in the speech of timber and horse.

Dominies

White is the January, and schoolboys' scuffed
Footprints in the snow lead to the sound of a bell.
It is Scotland and I attend the dead dominies.
A hand is spinning the globe, saying 'Galileo'
In a cold classroom, in a puff of chalk-dust.
Dominies, dead now, forgive these gauche lines,
My compromised parsings. Boyhood's grammarians
Set down the long examination, 'ink exercises'
At moments of mania, running riot through
The iron language like a trill of angry Rs.
'What sorts of men were the Caesars? Did you heave an axe,
At the wall, against them? Did you stand for your country?
Keep up with the translation. It is good for you.
Horace. Livy. Ballantyne. I am already historical.'

Witch-girl

For evermore, they said, that girl was lame
In hands and feet, and that, they said, was proof
The lightless Devil spelled her into horse,
Moulding her hands and feet in solid hoof.

Poor girl, her mother saddled her, then rode
Through Sutherland until the outraged Law
Attended to the giddy-ups of gossip,
Force-feeding both of them on Tolbooth straw.

Only her mother was condemned. A pious mob –
Citizens and presbyters – whinnied, neighed,
Clip-clopped, as, standing in their fear of God,
There too were men who watched but also pitied.

Cold day in Dornoch . . . Shivering, the witch
Relieved her freezing round that fire which burned
To burn her up. Crowds psalmed with horror.
She blistered in the tar and, screaming, burned.

They spoke in Dornoch how the horses mourned
And how that lame girl, wandering, was heard
Tearing at the grass; and how she sat and sang,
As if the Devil also made her bird;

And how she washed her lameness in the rivers
From Oykell to the Clyde and Tweed and Forth,
Notorious as something to be pitied,
A girl to look at but a beast in worth.

No one could see her but would think he saw
Hoof in her fumbling hands, her staggering gait.
They spurned her flowers, as if they'd grown from her;
They barbed their righteous charity with hate.

She hawked her flowers in Glasgow, by the Trongate;
In Edinburgh, selling flowers, she slept
Beside the braziers of the City Guard.
The earth and animals within her wept.

No one to help her; no one saw her die,
If she is dead. By Gryfe, by Deveron,
By Cree and Tay, I see her wash her lameness,
And hear her breathing in the wood and stone.

Washing the Coins

You'd start at seven, and then you'd bend your back
Until they let you stand up straight, your hands
Pressed on your kidneys as you groaned for lunch,
Thick sandwiches in grease-proofed bundles, piled
Beside the jackets by the hawthorn hedges.
And then you'd bend your little back again
Until they let you stand up straight. Your hands,
On which the earth had dried in layers, itched, itched,
Though worse still was that ache along the tips
Of every picking finger, each broken nail
That scraped the ground for sprawled potatoes
The turning digger churned out of the drills.
Muttering strong Irish men and women worked
Quicker than local boys. You had to watch them.
They had the trick of sideways-bolted spuds
Fast to your ear, and the upset wire basket
That broke your heart but made the Irish laugh.
You moaned, complained, and learned the rules of work.
Your boots, enlarging as the day wore on,
Were weighted by the magnets of the earth,
And rain in the face was also to have
Something in common with bedraggled Irish.
You held your hands into the rain, then watched
Brown water drip along your chilling fingers
Until you saw the colour of your skin
Through rips disfiguring your gloves of mud.
It was the same for everyone. All day
That bead of sweat tickled your smeared nose
And a glance upwards would show you trees and clouds
In turbulent collusions of the sky
With ground and ground with sky, and you portrayed
Among the wretched of the native earth.

[154]

Towards the end you felt you understood
The happy rancour of the Irish howkers.
When dusk came down, you stood beside the byre
For the farmer's wife to pay the labour off.
And this is what I remember by the dark
Whitewash of the byre wall among shuffling boots.
She knew me, but she couldn't tell my face
From an Irish boy's, and she apologized
And roughed my hair as into my cupped hands
She poured a dozen pennies of the realm
And placed two florins there, then cupped her hands
Around my hands, like praying together.
It is not good to feel you have no future.
My clotted hands turned coins to muddy copper.
I tumbled all my coins upon our table.
My mother ran a basin of hot water.
We bathed my wages and we scrubbed them clean.
Once all that sediment was washed away,
That residue of field caked on my money,
I filled the basin to its brim with cold;
And when the water settled I could see
Two English kings among their drowned Britannias.

Galloway Motor Farm

They spoil a farm, already written off
Against experience or income tax –
Two Land Rovers, several tractors,
These wooden cattle-floats like shanty huts;
A Jaguar, garaged in the air and grass,
On highways of self-heal and lady's bedstraw;
A Morris shooting-brake is bedded down
With agricultural gear and tackle.

Scattered beside derelict byres and barns,
Awkward, out of place, they lie here, eyesores
Cast out from progress, maladroitly banned
Machinery, discarded implements.
Wastrel existences, I can hear them
As each one wrestles free of function,
Picked over, plundered by who dumped them here,
Already scavenged for their feus of scrap.

The chemistry of weather has installed
Its scaffolding, from which it builds its rusts
On the iron of a horse-drawn reaper.
Air braces itself before stinging nettles.
Car doors, bumpers, bonnets, mudguards, engines –
Earth will not have them back until their steels,
Their chromes, veneers and leathers marry with
These stony contours as the brides of place.

I will be glad to have been here, living
Within this stung bubble where antiquities
Freshen, where they breathe the present tense.
Docken, yarrow, the muscular turf, ignore
These rubbished profits and spent wages.
It all means less than nothing to the bat
On his manic itinerary, and the fox
Was born too late to live with other landmarks.

As for a man, then he may walk beside
These thumbed-down vehicles, posing the moon
Against the window of a truck's high cabin;
Or sit inside, behind the wheel, thinking
A roadless countryside as he pretends
He's motoring through the night. Scotland, come back
From the lost ground of your dismantled lands.
A carelessness has defaced even the bluebell.

Tonight, by a steading, an iron reaper
That once outscythed the scythe
Is a silent cry of its materials,
With all its blunt blades yearning for the stone.
It has come from the yonside of invention,
From pulverable ore and foundry hammers.
Old harness rots above the rusted horseshoes.
Unborn horses graze on the back pastures.

Monumental Sculptor

That look on his face, consulting
His telephone directory,
Is a respectful smirk,
A shading of his dusty eyebrows.

Stooped round his left-hand grip
On a chisel, he is there to tell us
His hammered catalogue of names
Is the stone book of his town.

With lean, ridged muscles of
A man who works with stone,
He sculpts his alphabets
Of memory and consolation.

Notice the slow certainty
Of how his two apprentices
Come round to his likeness,
Inheriting his cut languages.

In the hut of his office
Are spiked invoices and a Bible.
He is in the fashion of God
In that black jacket he wears

When his customers call,
Holding his price-lists and designs,
Discussing the choice of words.
A kettle boils among the stone-dust.

I hear his phone ringing,
As, with a genuflecting crane,
Which squeaks of chains, of stretched links,
They hoist a finished page of marble.

There is no need to answer it,
Not in this trade. The name
Will still be there tomorrow
For his craft of the Kirk's loved ones.

The Harp of Renfrewshire

Contemplating a map

Annals of the trilled R, gently stroked L,
Lamenting O of local literature,
Open, on this, their one-page book, a still
Land-language chattered in a river's burr.

Small-talk of herdsmen, rural argument –
These soft disputes drift over river-meadows,
A darg of conversations, a verbal scent –
Tut-tutted discourse, time of day, word-brose.

Named places have been dictionaried in
Ground's secret lexicon, its racial moan
Of etymology and cries of pain
That slit a summer wind and then were gone.

A mother calls her daughter from her door.
Her house, my stone illusion, hugs its hill.
From Eaglesham west to the rocky shore
Her cry is stretched across bog-asphodel.

The patronymic miles of grass and weddings,
Their festivals of gender, covenants,
Poor pre-industrially scattered steadings,
Ploughed-up davochs – old names, inhabitants.

And on my map is neither wall or fence,
But men and women and their revenue,
As, watching them, I utter into silence
A granary of whispers rinsed in dew.

War Blinded

For more than sixty years he has been blind
Behind that wall, these trees, with terrible
Longevity wheeled in the sun and wind
On pathways of the soldiers' hospital.

For half that time his story's troubled me –
That showroom by the ferry, where I saw
His basketwork, a touch-turned filigree
His fingers coaxed from charitable straw;

Or how he felt when young, enlisting at
Recruiting tables on the football pitch,
To end up slumped across a parapet,
His eye-blood running in a molten ditch;

Or how the light looked when I saw two men,
One blind, one in a wheelchair, in that park,
Their dignity, which I have not forgotten,
Which helps me struggle with this lesser dark.

That war's too old for me to understand
How he might think, nursed now in wards of want,
Remembering that day when his right hand
Gripped on the shoulder of the man in front.

Savings

She saved her money
And she hid her money in
An oriental tin
That came from Twining's Tea.
– 'Oh, how much money have you now?'
But she'd never let me see.
She'd place that tin into my hands,
Then with her hands on mine
She'd help me shake her Twining's tin –
Half-crowns and a sovereign,
Shillings, sixpences and florins
Rattled on the paper notes.
That was her funeral fund
I was too young to understand.
When I did, and she was dead,
It wasn't death that I could see
In tea-leaves sifting from a spoon
That came out of a Chinese tin.
I saw the life she'd shovelled in.

Rose

So, little rose, it is all over
And you need no longer
Explore your cupped shapes,
Your fine organic enamels.

Four days you sat there
In a simple blue glass.
I watched you, I watched you;
I kept my eye on you.

My love is four days gone from me.
You have been good company.
I knew it would be like this –
You'd die the day of her return.

You have sat there in silence
Like a thought prayer.
You have been my good intentions.
You listened to me with patience.

Now I am in a gentle panic,
Not knowing what to do with you.
I will make up a ritual
For the departures of roses.

You will go into the heaven
Of unforgotten things.
Matisse will paint you;
Or Samuel Peploe will.

The door of her taxi is closing.
But you did not tell me your secrets.
I shall drink the water
Which did not preserve you long enough.

I will remember you in the French language.
I eat you now to keep you for ever.
Hello, my love. See?
This thorn has cut my lips.

Saturday

For Sandra and Chetwyn

Driving along the B1248
We pass such villages as Wetwang, or
North Grimston of descending Z-bends.
The Wolds are rolling for our benefit;
The long woods stride towards the eastern shore.
Frost sparks refrigerated ploughland to
A fan of silver ribs, good husbandry
In straight lines, going downhill to a point,
A misted earthen star, half-frost, half-ground.
And we are going to our country friends
At Kirkbymoorside, bearing a pineapple,
Some books of interest and a fine Bordeaux.
I wish it to be today, always, one hour
On this, the pleasant side of history.

Courting

On a summer's night to come
We'll find ourselves walking
Through a familiar Park.
I feel it happening –
Surprised anachronisms
In a delight, posed as
Hand-holding listeners to
Light overtures, percussed
From a lanterned bandstand
Through shaken foliage.

An autumn afternoon
Rehearses mist and brown
For a rediscovery –
That colour of angels
Flighted with chestnut leaves
Above the arrogant
Scarf-tightening waterfall,
A down-roar of water
Into the sinister
Conventional shadows.

It is already chosen,
A retrospective Sunday
When the still lake is glazed,
When bird-bread breaks underfoot,
Frost-toasted on cinder paths
And rhododendrons look
Snowed green exotica,
A botany of drips:
We will walk there again
With our white conversations.

Gardened from countryside,
The Park heaps love-days
On nature's edge; it is
An album of the Spring
In that season: woodland's
Municipal surprise,
Vernal formalities,
Mute orchestras of bluebells
When light leans on the leaf
And the thrush sings of rain.

Come with me now, dear girl,
And we will walk our years
Together. They open,
As gates do, or books, the heart's
Preliminary landmarks –
That path that leads nowhere
And a meadow beyond;
This path that leads into
Wilder greens of love,
A grass for walking on.

E. A. Walton thinks of painting
'The Daydream'

I kissed my sweet girl-cousins
One by one
Then they grew up
And I never saw them again.
They are lost among
Marriages and houses
At places where
The farms run out of fields
And towns begin.
I remember a girl
Who looked at her own future,
Lying among the flowers –
Milk-pail and butter-churn,
A belled cow led home
On a frayed halter.

The Local

Come, let us lower the tone, talking in
These smoky cadences and lounge-bar whispers.
We will enumerate the lost realia.
The Spirit of the Age will turn its back
And run away from such a narrative.
Notice how beer-mats slip a little on
These inconspicuous pools of slop and spillage.
It suggests half an epiphany is happening.
Or what else is it, tilting in my head,
Which makes me watch the sandwiches grow stale,
That slow bending of bread in Perspex bins
At the end of the bar? That, too, explains
A revolution or a crazed malaise
In the wink of a listening stranger.
I can hear music in the oiled hinges
When that door opens, a memory of
Unwritten Mozart or a lost Haydn
In the old man whistling in the Gents
Among the cisterns. Matisse emerges from
A doodled beer-mat; a fingernail engraves
An odalisque from a remembered girl
In a wet bar-counter's puddled drainage.
A man stands muttering his faulty tales
Of Burma in the last days of its Raj.
His eyes glint like a kukri in his dark
Leaf-hidden forays. 'Arakan,' he says,
To no one. 'Rajput. Frightened. Subahdar.'
The Empire ends here, in his anecdotes.
Now add to this the humming of an unplayed
Juke-box. Add chattering at corner tables.
You can hear what I mean in the whirred blades
Of the ventilator's recitations.

Its draughty epic is a literature
Depicting murky ale and tragic drunks
Who were lovers and heroes once, in days
No longer as these ones we live now among
Susurrations and vague moral endeavour.
I shall ingratiate myself with God,
Sticking it out in the land of the living.
Placebo Domino in regione vivorum.
The juke-box hammers out its antiphon.
They service it by feeding in new anthems.
And someone sings, a would-be dandy with
A withered buttonhole. My brain opens.
The streets are bathed in summer and a man
Who's five pence short of what a refill costs
Rejects the dandy's overstated affluence.
We could commune with our ancestors,
Whoever they were. We could talk of life
And death and poetry. We could be neutral,
Smiling with goodwill. Instead, we stand
In this armpit of English vernacular,
Hopelessly in touch with where we are.
The dead lie under our feet like pipelines.
The unacknowledged, counting pennies from
An outstretched palm, know what compassion's worth,
Here, humbly, off a High Street in the North.

Second-hand Clothes

A girl anoints a dress
With four silver coins.
Hands rinse among textiles,
Encountering others' skins.
Held up, observed for rips,
For their proximities
To new, to cleanliness,
To fit, their owners are
A hearsay of shapes, a bag
At these elbows, a button
Gone from this tight collar.
I think of all the feet
That walked in these shoes,
Toes down-pointing now from
A rail, each rail-held heel,
And each scuffed toe, caught in
The second-hand quadrille.
The strict proprietrix
Flicks ash on the bare floor.
The boards are a brushed dirt.
Even these women look
As taken off as shirts,
Worn sweaters, skirts, sea-boots,
And thrown down on a floor.
Coats, ranked on their hangers,
Pose – shamed vagrants, slaves
Whose prices she calls out
As you shuffle their shrugs.
And here a man may buy
One cufflink, scarves, or socks,
A glove, or soup-stained tie,
Or a large box of dust.

There could have been a war
Yesterday. I walk home,
A suitably ashamed
Observer of the poor;
And I wonder at the coins
On her watery tray,
By her pot-plants. What does
She wish for, having stood
So long by the red bars
Of her electric fire
In her shop, having seen
The fact of poverty
And served its enterprise
In England, arms folded,
Witnessing its shame,
Its sizes, dignity,
The hard, proud faces of
Regular customers,
Who buy, sell, delve into
Her tubs of washed-out thread?
A shabby drunk goes down
In a corner puddle.
When I got home, I crawled
Into my mouth, sat down,
And fell into a cloth sleep.
There's nothing to be done
Save follow the lost shoes.

Remembering Lunch

Noticing from what they talk about, and how they stand, or
    walk,
That my friends have lost the ability or inclination to wander
Along the shores of an estuary or sea in contented solitude,
Disturbs me on the increasingly tedious subject of myself.
I long for more chances to walk along depopulated shores,
For more hours dedicated to fine discriminations of mud
As it shades from grey to silver or dries into soft pottery;
Discriminations of wind, sky, rough grasses and
    water-birds,
And, above all, to be well-dressed in tweeds and serviceable
    shoes
Although not like an inverted popinjay of the demented
    gentry
But as a schoolmaster of some reading and sensibility
Circa 1930 and up to his eccentric week-end pursuits,
    noticing,
Before the flood of specialists, the trace of lost peoples
In a partly eroded mound, marks in the earth, or this and that
Turned over with the aforementioned impermeable
    footwear.
Describing this to my strangely sophisticated companions
Is to observe them docket it for future reference in
A pigeon-hole of the mind labelled *Possible Satires*.
We are far gone in our own decay. I admit it freely,
Longing no more for even the wherewithal of decent
    sufficiency
Or whatever hypothetical brilliance makes it possible.
Whatever my friends long for, they no longer confess it
In the afternoon twilight of a long lunch in London
After that moment when the last carafe has been ordered.
Such delicate conversations of years gone by! You would
    think

Perceptions of this sort best left for approaching senility,
Especially as, in my case, I was not born ever to expect
To enjoy so long-drawn-out a lunchtime at steep prices
Among tolerant waiters resigned to our lasting presences
As if they sense a recapitulation by young men of young
  men
In that fine hour of Edwardian promise at the *Tour Eiffel*
Or expatriate Americans and Irishmen in 'twenties Paris.
It is pretty well standard among literary phenomena.
Whether in the Rome of Marcus Martialis or London
  ordinaries
Favoured by roaring playwrights and poets destined for
Future righteousness or a destructive addiction to sack,
Lunch, lunch is a unitary principle, as Balzac would tell you
And as any man of letters consulting his watch towards
  noon
Would undoubtedly endorse. Lunch is the business of
  capitals,
Whether in *L'Escargot Bienvenue*, *Gobbles*, or the cheap Italian
  joint.
Impoverished or priggish in the provinces, where talent is
  born,
The angry poets look towards London as to a sea of
  restaurants,
Cursing the overpriced establishments of where they live
And the small scatter of the like-minded not on speaking
  terms.
But even this pleasure has waned, and its sum of parts –
People shaking hands on the pavement, a couple entering
A taxi hailed in the London rain, the red tears on a bottle
And the absorbing conspiracies and asserted judgements
Of young men in the self-confident flush of their promise –
Its sum of parts no longer presents a street of epiphanies.
Too much now has been spoken, or published, or
  unpublished.

Manias without charm, cynicism without wit, and integrity
Lying around so long it has begun to stink, can be seen and
    heard.
To come down south from the country in a freshly pressed
    suit
Is no longer the exercise in youthful if gauche dignity
It was once in days of innocent enthusiasm without routine.
And so I look forward to my tweed-clad solitude, alone
Beside a widening estuary, the lighthoused island
    appearing
Where waves of the sea turmoil against the river's waters
Baring their salty teeth and roaring. And here I can stand –
Forgive me my fantasies as, Lord, I surely forgive you
    yours –
In a pretence of being a John Buchan of the underdog,
With my waistcoated breast puffed against the wind. What
    do they long for?
Propping up bars with them I can pretend to be as they are
Though I no longer know what they are thinking, if ever I
    did,
And, raising this civil if not entirely sympathetic interest
In what they feel, I know it contributes little to them,
Adding, as it does, to a change in myself they might not
    notice,
Causing me this pain as I realize the way I must change
Is to be different from friends I love and whose company –
When the last carafe was ordered, an outrageous remark
    spoken,
Or someone announced his plan for an innovating stanza
Or a new development in his crowded sex-life – whose
    company
Was a landmark in my paltry accumulation of knowledge.
Perhaps, after all, this not altogether satisfactory
Independence of mind and identity before larger notions
Is a better mess to be in, with a pocketful of bread and cheese,

My hipflask and the *Poésie* of Philippe Jaccottet,
Listening to the sea compose its urbane wilderness,
Although it is a cause for fear to notice that only my
    footprints
Litter this deserted beach with signs of human approach,
Each squelch of leather on mud complaining, *But where are
    you going?*

Green Breeks

J. G. Lockhart, *Memoirs of Sir Walter Scott*,
Macmillan, 1900. Vol. 1, pages 81–5.

Crosscauseway, Bristo Street, and Potterrow,
In Edinburgh, seventeen eighty-three –
    Boys there were poor, their social class was 'low';
    Their futures lay in work or livery.
Sir Walter Scott says they 'inhabited'
These streets they lived on; but, in George's Square,
    'The author's father' – so Sir Walter said –
    Did not 'inhabit' but 'resided' there.
Young Walter and his chums were organized
Into a 'company' or 'regiment'.
    A 'lady of distinction', who despised
    The ragged street-boys from the tenements,
Gave Scott 'a handsome set of colours', which
Made Walter grateful to that Highland bitch
Who'd later 'clear' her kinsmen from her land,
That Duchess-Countess named for Sutherland.

From Potterrow, Crosscauseway, Bristo Street,
The poor boys came to 'bicker' on the Square –
    A military game, if indiscreet –
    To thrash the sons of those 'residing' there.
Offspring of State, Law, Ministry and Bank,
With flag aloft, defended their regime
    Against those 'chiefly of the lower rank',
    Boy-battles at a simplified extreme.
Though vanquished from the subtly written book
That's history, the street-boys often won –
    Scott says they did. Sir Walter undertook
    Average lies in how he wrote it down –
Mendacious annals – that no one should forget
When beggars win, they're in the horsemen's debt;
And only Scott has chronicled their war –
A beaten boy becomes the conqueror.

One of his enemies, says Scott, was both
Ajax and Achilles of the Crosscauseway –
    'The very picture of a youthful Goth' –
    The first to fight and last to run away.
Blue-eyed, with long fair hair, tall, finely made,
That boy-barbarian awed him. Scott could tell
    He and his class-mates mustered to degrade
    This brave, presumptuous, vulgar general.
They called him Green Breeks, this boy whom Scott
    preserved
As a memento of his opposite
    That, cheating him of what he led and served,
    A novelist could have his way with it.
Scott draws the colour of his hero's eyes,
His shape, his height, but not the boy, who dies
Within the pickle of Scott's quickened prose,
Half-loved by Scott, half-feared, born to oppose.

In one fight, Green Breeks laid his hands upon
Sutherland's 'patrician standard'. Before
    He'd time to win it, he was faced with one
    Too zealous for 'the honour of the Corps'
Who had a hanger or *couteau de chasse*.
For honour, then, that boy cut Green Breeks down.
    To save a flag, the honour of his class,
    He struck him on the head and cut him down.
Imagined horsemen of the old regime
Transformed young Green Breeks to a Dying Gaul –
    A pictured history, the bronze of dream,
    A classic gesture in an urban brawl.
Scott's friend disgraced his 'regiment' and showed
Expedient dragoonship was its code.
Where was nobility? But Scott, you found
Your life's obsession on that cobbled ground.

Scott turned our country round upon its name
And time. Its history obeyed his whip
    When Scott sent out his characters to claim
    Their pedigrees in Green Breeks' leadership.
I do not understand, Scott, what you meant
By your displaced verse-prose 'nobility'
    Unless the tatters of your 'regiment'
    Were patched on Green Breeks, that, for chivalry,
Your heroes might go forth and look the part –
Part man, part prince, part soldier and part God –
    Ridiculous and lacking in support
    As, when they fall, mere modern men applaud.
But Scott, you failed; for where your Green Breeks lives
Is that dark tenement of fugitives
Who, fled from time, have no need to endure
The quicklime of your ordered literature.

Green Breeks did not inform. He kept his pride.
He nursed his lovely grudge and sword-cracked skull
    And took both pain and bribery in his stride.
    They offered cash, 'smart money', to annul
Shame and dishonoured laws. He would not sell
His wound: let them remember it. Scott says
    That childish purse was small – part comical,
    Part serious: the whole antithesis.
They would not meet him face to face, but stood
On dignity and used a go-between,
    Like states, transacting with the multitude,
    Who can negotiate, then intervene
With laws, with cavalry and troops, with style,
With system, representatives and guile,
Who, pompously, can compromise to win,
Pitch coins against a ragged ostentation.

Peasant baroque, like this, its nuts screwed tight
In praise of rabbles and those *sans culottes*,
    Won't change a thing. It whets an appetite,
    Unfankling truths inwoven like a knot.
It gestures like a ghost towards a ghost,
And, bringing Green Breeks back, or trying to,
    It reckons with desire, the human cost
    In losing what was old, and fierce, and true.
What did he do? Where did he live, and die?
That life can be imagined. I let him *be*.
    He is my light, conspirator and spy.
    He is perpetual. He is my country.
He is my people's minds, when they perceive
A native truth persisting in the weave
Of shabby happenings. When they turn their cheeks
The other way, he turns them back, my Green Breeks.

Green Breeks accepted what he asked them give –
A pound of snuff for 'some old woman – aunt,
    Grandmother, or the like', with whom he lived.
    Kindness, like courtesy, must ever haunt
Love-raddled reminiscence, Walter Scott.
You cannot hide behind mock-epic prose
    Your love of 'haves', amusement at 'have-nots'.
    Between your lines, it's easy to suppose
Deeper affections generate each word
Recalling Green Breeks in your years of fame.
    You drank toasts to his name in Abbotsford,
    Proposed to Green Breeks, not his father's name.
Be not amused, Scott. Go, and give him thanks
He let you patronize his 'lower ranks'.
Go, talk to him, and tell him who you are,
Face to face, at last, Scott; and kiss his scar.

Tannahill

Robert Tannahill, 1774–1810

'I would I were a weaver, I could sing all manner of songs.'
Shakespeare

Aye, Bobbie Tannahill, I'll brew
Unhappy truths of verse and you
In Scots lines of the turn and screw.
    Aye, Tannahill,
This reckoning is overdue,
    Lamentable.

We sang your songs in Paisley's school,
Ink-fingered Dux and classroom fool,
Each little lord of ridicule;
    Aye, Tannahill,
All learned your sweet and bountiful
    Melodic drill.

By singing you, I understood
That poetry's lax brotherhood
Lived in my town; and it was good –
    Aye, Tannahill –
To learn that verse did not exclude
    A local skill.

Blackboyds and yeltrins in the year
Seventeen hundred and seventy-four
Were ripe and brilliant, born to dare
    'The sin of rhyme'
That Burns committed in his pure
    Intimate crime.

In seventeen hundred and eighty-six
They set you learn a weaver's tricks
While Burns discovered Muses vex
    As well as grace,
Young Burns, whose Scots proprietrix
    Spat in his face.

Douce dandies of the posh salons
Took that man in, as if on loan,
Then having raised, they laid him down,
    Their ploughman poet.
They made Society's decision,
    And let him know it.

Burns, Tannahill and Fergusson,
These jorum-jirgers, they could hone
A merry R, lick till they shone
    Gently stroked Ls,
And then die young, or in Darien,
    Ink's asphodels.

Young dead like Leyden, Smith and Gray,
Unread, forgotten, sternly weigh
Against the doors of elegy
    And find them shut.
Timor mortis conturbat me –
    Not to forget.

An antiquarian of old airs,
You played your flute at Renfrew's fairs;
You sang of amorous despairs
    And country courting.
Aye, Tannahill, hurt love confers
    A sweeter singing.

[183]

Composing verses at your bench,
Lines woven inch by linen inch
To follow each iambic hunch
    Into its art,
You sang, like a beginning finch,
    Your common heart.

A wabster's craft would teach a man
To live with art as an artisan.
As you could weave, teach me to scan
    And turn a rhyme,
Fraternally, like Caliban
    His low sublime.

When Paisley's bodies sought to learn
At the Star Inn and the Sun Tavern,
You, Tannahill, taught them discern
    False verse from true.
They 'kenned y'r faither', and would turn
    Their wits on you.

Once set in print, that was enough;
Your melodies had had their puff,
Their papery chance. With each rebuff
    Your inkwells dried;
You, Tannahill, in local chaff,
    Were vilified.

My Tannahill, the delicate
Delight of poetry is to wait
And, suffering the alphabet,
    Allow songs come
The way a prodigal in debt
    Walks slowly home.

You could not wait, yet overheard
A fame that rarely is conferred –
Anonymously choristered,
    A song you wrote;
A farm-girl, singing as she sheared,
      Your song, her throat.

And still they are singing, by Gryfe,
By Cart, with gentle disbelief
In the lilt of words against life;
    And your words breathe
In the pianos, with a little laugh,
      Keeping their faith.

Gone, gone down, with a song, gone down,
My Tannahill. The tavern town
Said one book was your last and frowned.
    The River Cart
Ran deep and waste where you would drown,
      Your counterpart.

You clutched the papers of your tongue:
Gone, gone down, gone down with a song.
Pity the mad, darkened with wrong.
    Home Lycidas,
You died in the dish-cloth Cart, among
      The ugliness.

And in the morning schoolboys came
To fish for papers, speak your name
And take their landed catches home,
    Dried on the gorse;
Aye, Tannahill, boys caught your poems,
      Lost, watery verse.

[185]

By broom, by briar, by Craigie Wood,
Through Cart-side's river neighbourhood,
Your papers rotting on the mud,
    My Tannahill!
But the shelfie and the hawthorn bud
    You could not kill.

John Wilson in Greenock, 1786

That day I stood before our magistrates
And minister, I hushed my heart's debates
With words and scenery, for I agreed
To let these pious dumplings intercede
Against my heard-of and once-printed *Clyde*
Which they thought damned, and I thought sanctified
Sights I had seen of water, wood and stone.
They took me, for I promised to abandon
'The profane and unprofitable art'
Of poetry. Swans sail, kingfishers dart
In colours of the fourteen halcyon days:
To think of them engenders miseries
In this man bonded to his self-disgust.
I read my *Clyde* as an unwritten ghost.
   I dreamt of living by the breath of fame,
A matter most opprobrious to them
Who pay me govern, according to their rule,
The wastrel brats of Greenock's Grammar School.
For the sake of my family, I waste
What once I loved, and hope to see disgraced
My living mind, which, for a stipend, closed
Itself on life and what life once proposed
Along the river-banks I loved and walked –
My classic verse shut tight, my heart unlocked.
What can I do but curse this pen, this hand
That's paid to cultivate the sterile sand
Of worthless juveniles? They know me for
My whipping tawse, and as ambassador
From fantasy, where I, their Master, write
Five-beat iambic artifice, contrite
No more, high-placed and able to afford
The only breaking of my written word

It would not break my heart to break – my name,
Myself. John Wilson, Master, will reclaim
John Wilson, poet, his being and his soul,
From contracts binding him to the control
Of ministers and moralists whose teeth,
He hopes, will fester in their Godly breath
And, rotted on their speech, will fall, to skid
Beneath the brogues of others *unco guid*.

By Nethan's banks, I first took up my pen
To lift our Lowland snipe and water-hen
Into Arcadia from Lanarkshire.
I walked them all, Gryfe, Cart and Douglas Water,
By Avon, Calder and by Elvan-Clyde
Where my half-tutored art was fortified
By waterfalls where Clyde is young and free,
As I was then, in that complicity
Clyde worked with verse. This was the way of it,
That I, John Wilson, Master, scholar, poet,
Would come to sign my name in hunger on
Vouchsafements of my own obscure damnation.

A nobleman, whom I beseeched, was pleased
To praise my poem, and see my troubles eased.
But then he died, before he could convert
His word to what I needed most, a shirt,
One pair of breeks, a bench, and pen and ink,
A room near water, and sweet time to think.
He tried, in jest, with guns, to frighten me,
Testing my courage or tenacity;
And what I swallowed then did me no good
As, penniless, I tasted livelihood,
Salt on my tongue, and sweat within my throat,
My life reduced to future anecdote.

In several mishandled interviews
I talked my gifts away, while their abuse,
To me, and poetry, earned me my bread,

Which I was glad of, for, a table, spread
Before a wife and children, is not greed,
And, knowing love, is somehow to succeed,
At least at home. Therefore, I dropped my pen
To teach Latinity in Rutherglen,
For what it was worth. I was disguised.
Each night I dreamt of fame as I revised
My praised and printed *Clyde*. I paid my rent
On every week of that imprisonment.
I paid my way, but what I could not buy
Was time enough to work and versify
The river of my mind into its soul,
Its pure alluded water, pool and fall,
Through birkenshaw, past steadings, with the grace
A classic metre grafts on native place.
For this, crude kirkmen treat me to contempt.
They do not know the harmony I dreamt
In days of promises I could not keep.
Too many obstacles, the rivers deep –
I could not climb or cross, but slaved instead
To see my wife, myself, my children fed.
Too many patriarchs and ministers
Between my Muse and me, that rose of hers
Soon crushed beneath the booted patriarchs –
A Renfrew rose, an Ayrshire rose, or Lanark's.
Wild rose and briar, tormentil and broom,
I see you through a coward's nom-de-plume,
And make this promise now, that once again
I'll draw you on the metres of my pen
To beats of which I dandle my own true
Love-children on the days I think of you.
Dear rivers, know, and see, your poet nurse
His children on his love's pentameters.
    That men with leisure, brave, or cunning, wise
Or ruthless men, might make the sacrifice

[189]

Is why I write this now, to take my chance
They'll blame my misdemeanours on finance
But note my tears, and know I broke my heart
For this profane, unprofitable art.
I see a rose, but am forbidden it.
I see a swan, but must not mention it.
I see a ruin, but I must not confer
Discarded history with music's whirr.
I see a stream, but I must not discern
A heathen Georgic in a Lowland burn.
Come, pity my embezzled universe,
My thwarted bestiary and guilty purse
As, high up on Greenock at the windy jaws
I hear again the literate applause
Of Elvan Water chattering to me
Its small-talk of polite society;
Or Cora Linn, in its delicious spate,
Delinquent, plunging and importunate.
A life ago I saw in Cadzow's bull
Europa and the Thunderer annul
The moral average, and once I saw
Naiads at Lanark, where the birkenshaw
Throws shadows on a water that acclaims
These pagan ladies at their water-games.
And one has come to us from Ayrshire's sod
Who jests at Kirks and outmanoeuvres God.
So tell them this, them, and their kind who set
My bond and oath before me, the alphabet
They cannot thole to hear as melody
Will do them down as sure as they downed me
Unless they learn a way of blotting truth
And shut his mouth, and shut his singing mouth
As they imprisoned mine, and dispossess
His art with purchased righteousness.
Buy and subvert that wanton, better man,

Profane, unprofitable citizen!
   With teaching – wed, my fame and art cut short;
With bitterness and nine bairns to support –
I earn my bread, a fugitive from song
Who measures wordless verses on his tongue
And keeps his word. I walk into the night
With beer and brandy for my appetite
Pretending my dismantled Muse deplored
The leisure which my purse could not afford.
From my mistakes and harbour tavern grog
I count my country in a catalogue
Of native vomits at the Clyde's sick mouth
Where brutish skippers mock me for my truth.
What consolation is it, what amends,
I live now where my mighty river ends?
Salt wilderness erupts from pastorals
At this Hesperides, and the sky falls
Where ocean's mercantile and cold Firth-tide
Confronts the country waters from the Clyde?
   I suffer wordlessly, as if the King
Or Ministers of State forbade me sing;
As if by seeming far from God and thrift
There was a blameless treason in my gift.
Those who come after me, whose mouths are shut,
Abandon tricks of *if, perhaps* and *but*,
And sign no bonds, but claim that *to be free*
Is carried on the back of poetry.
Blame me, if you must blame me; and say my will
Was feeble-weak, and then contemptible;
That in the theatres of verse, my *Clyde*
Draws no applause. But know, I worked, and tried;
And hope still for a small posterity
And, through a chink in time, to hear men say,
That, wasting these best talents of my life,
I fed my children and I loved my wife.

[191]

La Route

A poem-film, starring Jean-Paul Belmondo

Whether or not the man driving
Is really my chauffeur – he is
A pal who happens to like caps –
Is unlikely, at this speed, to
Bother anyone we pass on
These country roads.
        This is the speed
We go at: illegible notices,
A gate half-open to a lane
Where . . . Hand on a shutter that's . . .
Someone's jumping off a tower
On a château that's blinked by sun.
No. It's a child who's throwing
Newspapers out of a window.
Is it? Why is he doing that?
Swift dapples of lime-shade are
Left behind, cool places for *boule*,
Old men who shuffle in the dust.
A silent weir; a fisherman
Snapped in the frame of pouring out
His glugless wine . . .
        And in here it's
Smoke, which has no words, despite mouths
Blowing it out; and no one wonders
Out there in the houses, up there
In the villas which have survived
The holidays and good times of
Their smart owners, that inside here
Is a man sitting on the back-seat
Notorious for fifty crimes,
For whom old peasant women in

Their hats are a multitude of
His own mother and several aunts;
Or that the young men in cafés –
Blurred, talking – are as fragile straws
He wishes he could catch with his eyes.
For I need to be one of them
Again, and stripped entirely clean
Of infidelity, this silk,
This speed and all that I have done.
These obsolete advertisements,
Each populated hole in the shade . . .
And it is not anonymous
Even at this speed which can make
A cigarette seem longer, or
The radio a function of
Travelling, a voice of nowhere
And no one at a microphone.
The seat's leather is heating up;
An open book is fast asleep.
She has left her hairbrush. It is
Rocking gently in a corner of
The hot back-seat. To take it back
Would not be gallantry, but
A waste of petrol. So why did
She choose to remain there, with them?
Nadine . . . Ruthless and beautiful:
She looks like both ideals. It is
A better trip without her; she, she . . .
How many women have I known?
If only, Nadine, you were not a liar . . .
That boy in the nylon overalls
Who is . . . that little bridge; these trees;
These children on stilts. She would have
Turned the radio up, too loud,
And chattered like the tart she was,

A fishwife slimmed for luxury,
A swimming-pool girl, a girl made by
Advertisements, my kind of girl
Who tastes of other men's champagne.
I doze like an open book, open,
Where my real life is written, told,
Told and shown, lying in two halves
And hinged, so, like the door I did
Not go through; and I think I am
A man who had no mother, who,
Therefore, is bad, and going to
A city where Max is standing
In a doorway, thinking that life
Is a dandy with a flick-knife
And a certain self-confidence
In clever cuts with it – up-cut,
Into the belly, and throat-cut,
For the kill. He thinks I don't know.
I know who paid him kill you, Jean.
I know he told you it was me,
But it wasn't, and you knew it.
Why, friend, do I weaken before
This dutiful revenge, as if
I've had enough, and this the last?
We are passing the houses of
Doctors and Professors. Sight
Is not what it was on this journey.
Max I see more clearly as
An executioner, or, if
Not that, then, at least, destiny
Who stands well-dressed in a shadow;
And faces, certainly, are not
So beautiful, nor are gardens
Anything like what I have seen
Today, with all the little quirks

People share, twitches, quarrels, food,
Their affections, their crazed sweetness
Accusing me. So, it is true:
There is a deep hole in the world.
Friend, you were with me, under the trees,
That summer we decided to reap
The pious franc instead of hay.
We did it with laughter. We were *good*.
It's a long road back; there were thefts
Conducted in the name of Law
Everywhere along it, making me
Almost a good man, who, sunk
In the ghost of my personality
Cannot remember my last drink
Or when I lit this cigarette.
It could have been years ago
Before the multitudes of mothers.
'Try a schoolmistress. She'll mother you.'
You used to say that, Jean, teasing me.
I aged like a ballad, always young.
No matter what I did, or thought,
An innocence clung to me like
A skin, a lime-shade, or like hair:
A history of love and theft,
Those deals; a history of suits
And big tips left in restaurants,
The career of my machismo –
Never stuck for a dame, or lost
For introductions to the rich.
Why, Jean, do they like crooks so much
In France? What's wrong with honesty?
A long road, Jean, but I never met
Anyone like me; I never met
Myself among the handshakes.
Max, I am coming to get you,

[195]

But, you bastard, if you stick me
It will be just as well, for I
Have seen a big hole in the world
That's full of paymasters, and you,
And I know what you don't, which is
That I'll go back the way I came
As safely on this leather seat,
Unnoticed in a machine, driven
By a black-capped chauffeur who says
Nothing, who, whatever happens,
Either way, Max, will take me home,
Who will have the good sense to know
Where, in the country, that is.

The Gallery

See, how this lady rises on her swing
Encouraged by the brush of Fragonard,
As light as love, as ruthless as the Czar,
Who, from her height, looks down on everything.

When on a canvas an oil-eye of blue
Has tiny fissures, you can stand behind,
Imagine time, observe, and condescend,
Wink at and spit on those who are not you.

Out of the eye of Christ, you might see God;
Or, from your swing, see pastoral machines
Romanticized, re-made as guillotines;
Or, Goya's captive, face a firing-squad;

Or, Goya's soldier, be condemned to hear
Eternity in the museum of death –
Your moment after triggering – and with
The horror of aesthetics in your ears.

Ah, they were lucky, who were drawn from life
By river-banks in summer, in café scenes,
The way they were, for all their speechless pains,
That absinthe drinker and his sober wife.

The Deserter
Homage to Robert Desnos

'Somewhere in the world, at the foot of an embankment,
A deserter parleys with sentries who don't understand his
   language.'

At the world's end, just before everything stops,
There may not be a war going on, but it is where
Broken lines of contested frontiers converge,
Drawn long ago by the hands of shrewd statesmen
In the years when they bagged the knees and elbows of
   their suits
In the grandest of all the world's capital cities.

It is at this place they keep the railway carriages
Of armistice and treaties, those waggons which brought
The revolutionary and his bales of pamphlets.
Many cattle trucks rot on a spread of sidings
With their memories of last kisses, of goodbyes,
A child's hand in yours, his eyes under the skip of his cap.

This is the last mortuary, the bottom inch of six feet,
Home to pallid garrisons sustained on cigarettes
And fantasies of strangers, wrapped in greatcoats
The way the inflexible uphold their ideologies.
Their freezing breath fastens them as if by chains
To a heaven above the arc-lamps, above innocent airliners.

Snow has begun to fall on the guilty secrets of Europe.
Here, where the lines meet, and emplacements rise up
Out of mined earth in their laurels of wire, a man,
Unarmed, talks with another five who hold their guns
On him. This conversation is composed of cloth,
Of buttons, stars, and boots. Of wood. Of steel. Of wire.

'A spectre in a well-tailored shroud
Smoked a cigar at the window of his apartment.'

We have seen him, this upright father
Who has the stately manners of a priest,
Who, when he lets it slip, behaves like a tycoon
In armaments, believing that they died
In Buchenwald for capitalism, for him.

We have dined with this stranger, talked at meat
With him after the funerals of our fathers.
Our wives are fond of him. They have been known to
Abscond to some Swiss chalet with him where
He keeps the instruments of pleasure.

How confidently the ash balances on
The tip of his cigar, a grey drool;
And with what contempt for his possessions
He lets it fall . . . We have seen him in cafés,
Served, as if he has only to wave his hand.

We are asked to die for him, and we die.
In the unlikeliest places, we have died,
Places we never dreamt of sending postcards from.
There, in his red resorts, men vanish in
Factories that grind through men and native parishes.

Never to die, not even in the grand style
Tended by nieces married to Counts and Princes,
But to live always, at the concept of wealth,
In galleries and in the regularity of verse,
In metronomes pledged to custom,

And in the regulation of wages and bread,
Never to die. O with how much passion
We can condemn this man many have died for.
He claims even to love nature.
He praises its brutality as he hunts.

In his mouth is the taste of Europe,
Its rank saliva. When I see this ghost,
I am afraid of him, who, from his window,
Spits on the lives of so many people,
On my mother, my father, my wife, my friends, myself.

'A widow in her wedding-gown gets into the wrong train.'

> So much is average, so much
> That anyone can buy or touch,
> Things you can watch, or put to sleep,
> That walk, or run on wheels, or creep.
>
> Other things are just mistaken,
> Marriages, or wrong trains taken.
> A widow in her wedding-gown
> Alights somewhere, in the wrong town.
>
> O Lady, run, it's over now,
> Whatever grief that marked your brow
> With something like a brilliant star
> To tell this city who you are.
>
> I shall possess your soul, bereaved
> Of everything for which it lived.
> I am a specialist of tears.
> I weep the world's, let me weep yours.

I listen to the song you sing
About two lives, two wedding-rings.
I listen as you fold your dress
To the mute curves of your nakedness.

Lamp-posts

You find them in the cities of Europe,
Ornate plush iron, stooped, fluted, winged,
And in the postures of old *boulevardiers*.
They stand outside hotels and embassies
As the commissionaires of *savoir faire*
And architecture, dressed in an era
Along the fashionable avenues.
In Paris like the ghosts of Baudelaire,
And in Prague like a street of Kafkas,
They contemplate the shadows round their feet.
Throw them a coin or two, for they are beggars
Touting beneath electric epaulettes
For the recovery of time, for hooves,
For carriages and footmen, or for her
Habsburgian slipper fallen in a pulse
Of gas-light and an equerry kneeling
To fit the slipper to its royal foot.
The rehabilitated lamps of Warsaw
Have been hung with civilians, improvised
As gallows while the multitudes of death
Marched over the rubble, in the darkness.
Therefore I mourn these uprooted lamp-posts
That lean against a wall, in a corner of
This warehouse, bleak, municipal, leaning
In stances of exhaustion, their arms across
Their eyes, their brows against a bare brick wall.

Loch Music

I listen as recorded Bach
Restates the rhythms of a loch.
Through blends of dusk and dragonflies
A music settles on my eyes
Until I hear the living moors,
Sunk stones and shadowed conifers,
And what I hear is what I see,
A summer night's divinity.
And I am not administered
Tonight, but feel my life transferred
Beyond the realm of where I am
Into a personal extreme,
As on my wrist, my eager pulse
Counts out the blood of someone else.
Mist-moving trees proclaim a sense
Of sight without intelligence;
The intellects of water teach
A truth that's physical and rich.
I nourish nothing with the stars,
With minerals, as I disperse,
A scattering of quavered wash
As light against the wind as ash.

Ode to a Paperclip

When I speak to you, paperclip, urging you
To get a move on and metamorphose,
You sit there mating with the light that shines
Out of your minerals, a brighter glint
Where, rounding at a loop, you meet the sun.
Paperclip, I like you, I need you.
Please, turn into something wonderful.

    I remember restless clerks, in boring places,
Unbend you to caress their ears, tickling
Their lobes, or, slowly, linking you until
They forged one of their office necklaces –
A daisy-chain, from flowers of the desk;
Or straighten you, to dab at inky fluff
Mossed round a comma or an asterisk.

    You have more uses than your name pretends.
Intimately fingered all late afternoon,
Frustrations weave you into metal knots,
Boredom's insignia in the typing-pools.
A secretary, composed but fidgeting,
Was once chastised with airborne paperclips,
But no one noticed what was being thrown.

    A box of you, when brought up from the store,
Then opened, looked at, looks like dying sprats,
All life in its pathetic multiples.
But these are not your proper transformations.
Who knows what purpose you'll be made to serve
When a suspender is in deep crisis, or
The manager's braces tear his buttons off?

    It's you they think of first, because they know
Your versatility can be delivered
On bodice straps or snapped elastics.
It's your neutrality that gets me down –

Disarming. Why do you do it? You work
On dictats to the underlings of death
As readily as you fasten up the drafts
   A democrat compiles on human rights.
Good and/or bad, important/unimportant –
Little survivor, you go where you're sent,
On memoranda from the Chiefs of Staff
To Ministers of State, down to the note
A man finds clipped inside his wage packet,
Saying, *Sorry, you've been made redundant.*
   You also get lost and nobody cares.
It's part of your status to turn up in
A handful of change, or to appear from
Her handbag when she's powdering her nose.
You've no prestige at all, a tiny one
Among the commonplace, the vacuumed millions,
Diminished things, the meek disposables.
   Hand-made gold-plated paperclips do not,
I am sure of it, get made, let alone
Presented at executive goodbyes,
Although I've seen a breasty typist wear you
As earrings and, on her, you looked like treasure.
More than familiars, more than desk-top trinkets,
You're precious, though we may not choose to say so.
   Give them gold watches or cut-glass decanters,
It's you they're likely to remember as
The days go by, watched from their patios,
As, too, they think of Miss-What-Was-Her-Name –
Evasive, leggy and impertinent –
The one who worked gymnastic, sculptural
Designs in wire, her secretarial art.
   Ubiquitous, docile and mass-produced,
Existing in relationship to work
And tedium expressed thereof, you are
As functional as roads or pen and ink.

A box of you, when shaken on the ear,
Can make Brazilian noises, a rhythmic sea,
Plural as salt, as leaves, as citizens.
    Ghost-bullets, triple-loops, no matter what
Inquiring minds might call your outline capsules,
You change your shapes and will go anywhere,
Do anything for a piece of the action.
Immoralist! Turncoat! Mercenary!
You don't need her, or him – Love me; love me,
And go where I go, gentle talisman.

Ratatouille

I

Consider, please, this dish of ratatouille.
Neither will it invade Afghanistan
Or boycott the Olympic Games in a huff.
It likes the paintings of Raoul Dufy.
It feeds the playboy and the working-man.
Of wine and sun it cannot get enough.
It has no enemies, no, not even
Salade niçoise or phoney recipes,
Not Leonid Brezhnev, no, not Ronald Reagan.
It is the fruits of earth, this ratatouille,
And it has many friends, including me.
Come, lovers of ratatouille, and unite!

II

It is a sort of dream, which coincides
With the pacific relaxations called
Preferred Reality. Men who forget
Lovingly chopped-up cloves of *ail*, who scorn
The job of slicing two good peppers thinly,
Then two large onions and six aubergines –
Those long, impassioned and imperial purples –
Which, with six courgettes, you sift with salt
And cover with a plate for one round hour;
Or men who do not care to know about
The eight ripe *pommes d'amour* their wives have need of,
Preparing ratatouille, who give no thought to
The cup of olive oil that's heated in
Their heaviest pan, or onions, fried with garlic
For five observant minutes, before they add
Aubergines, courgettes, peppers, tomatoes;
Or men who give no thought to what their wives

Are thinking as they stand beside their stoves
When seasoning is sprinkled on, before
A *bouquet garni* is dropped in – these men
Invade Afghanistan, boycott the Games,
Call off their fixtures and prepare for war.

III

Cook for one hour, and then serve hot or cold.
Eat it, for preference, under the sun,
But, if you are Northern, you may eat
Your ratatouille imagining Provence.
Believe me, it goes well with everything,
As love does, as peace does, as summers do
Or any other season, as a lifetime does.
Acquire, then, for yourselves, ingredients;
Prepare this stew of love, and ask for more.
Quick, before it is too late. *Bon appétit!*

from Europa's Lover

'Our Europe is not yours.'
– Camus

'Men make more than one native land for themselves.
There are some who feel at home in twenty corners of
the world, for men are born more than once.'
– Nizan

I

That beautiful lady walked
To the fragrant terrace
Of an especial hotel.
She walked out of the dusk
With Europe on her arm.

'Where are your shoes, Lady?
And your gown of silk,
This subtle décolletage,
Could not have been designed
In our provincial spa.'

'No,' she said. 'When my
Impeccable maternity
Concluded, my last child buried,
I had this made in Paris
By surrealist seamstresses.'

'Listen,' she said – you know
That listening tilt,
That smile on hearing far music? –
'These are the saxophones,
Far away, of the Riviera.'

'Sit by me,' said the Lady.
'You will suffer and travel
Thousands of years with me
Through my archives of sun and rain,
My annals of rivers and earth.'

II

'First, you must lose that obsession,'
She said, 'which deals in
Survival, prosperity and salvation.'

She showed me the waters of invitation,
Deep springs that coughed clear in the ground,
More solicitous than those
Thin, thermal pools, sipped at,
Bathed in and bottled in our matronly spa.

Debts were hushed in the bureaucracies.
Watery sunlight was a burst
Lit improvisation of liquid.
She scattered flowers on the water,
The mistress of her own rituals.

'Now you have died once, you will die again,
And live again. At your own funerals
You will stand among the trees
And grieve for your progeny and future selves.'

III

Cold scholars in a christendom,
We are the children of children.
When was it in traditions that
We stopped living? When did we die?

Scriptoria furniture,
Oaken tables, oaken panels,
A trapped butterfly fluttering
Among the pedantry and heresies
In chained tomes, in motes of heart-dust . . .
An introspective summer illuminates
Tinted stories on the windows,
The gossip in the history of glass.
A narrative of colours spreads
On the blond stone, coagulated
Medieval light ruminating
Like abstract detectives on the slabs.
Lucid difficulties murmur
Contemplative stories of the West,
Martyrdoms, Reformations, Schisms.
Those finely carved mottoes
In delicate Latin are fading
As timber grows again
In a scriptorium bursting into leaf.
One more rub of an elbow,
Another scholar at this desk
Will return it to nature.
The inscriptions will float away
To Byzantine fastnesses
Or an islanded Irish hermitage.

IV

Many times we have risen
From the earthen delicatessen
Of the cemeteries, to tread
Moistened dust on city streets
Among litter, hand in hand,
Increasingly démodé, disappearing
Into salutations of light and water
At the foot of elaborate gardens
Where leaves are burned
In a dusk-rinsed smoke.

We are at home by nocturnal taxi ranks,
By the fast-food carts and chestnut hawkers
Ragged beside charcoal braziers
In these corners of metropolitan warmth.
We are at home among dandies
On the steps of the Opera House,
Among the crimson titles at passing-out parades
Or on the corners of unmapped rural lanes
Where wind meets us with a smell of cattle
And the scent of future rain.
We are at home in any occasion of
Citizens, urbanal and pastoral.

V

'What walks we have taken, together on
The verge of revealing our secrets,'
She said to me, incognito among
Market-stalls around a cathedral.

'We have seen the light-hearted
At their moderate courtships,
Whether pointing to the erotic stars
Or to the obese, detestable Zéppelins.

'In the fire-storms, love survived
And the terrorized hugged each other
To an inward collapse of hot char.
Silver birds of Imperial Airways flew

'From India with citizens and dossiers,
With brides flying to their weddings
High above the deserts, seas and ranges,
And even long armies and ferocious machines

'Failed to transform our favoured places,
And cruelty dies in the heart.
Still they come flying, and we welcome the dead
As they arrive to us in their wedding-clothes.'

VI

Shaped into this intimate suffering of death with life,
Past with present, living beneath a succession of coats
Until skin thickens into cloth, thread and blood, coarse
    immortality,
And blood thickens, and words melt on your tongue
As gourmet as a peppermint on a plate at Maxim's;
Shaped on a field behind the plough you were born to,
Shaped to these footprints, this size, in a drawing-room
Where you must sing before a brother of the bishop
Because aunt tells you to through her mouthful of cake;
Shaped as you sweep the gutter of its rejected trash –
How lonely is litter! – shaped as you sign a treaty
With the usurping nephew of a Maharajah or a Czar's
Bomb-crazy ambassador or a Kaiser's confidant;
Shaped before furnaces or dragging coal-carts with your
    back
In the mines of Yorkshire or Silesia, or shaped,
Shaped and indentured in the gardens of rhododendrons,
    peacocks
And exotic flora brought home by an eccentric uncle
Who commanded the firing-squads at Brazzaville or
    Hyderabad;
Shaped by decks and masts, spits and spars, that twiggery
Sprouting from warehouses before the continental
    wharves;
Shaped by regiment; shaped by evictions, shaped by
Rhetorical prelates and their torturing sectaries;
Shaped in the moulds of foundries in Glasgow and
    Düsseldorf,
From cleared crofts in Sutherland to Fontamara, shaped,
Shaped, shaped and ruled, in kingdoms and palatinates, by
    archon,

By tyrant, by imperial whim gathering spiderwebs
To please Heliogabalus, by parliament, by Bourbon, by
    Tudor,
By Stuart, by Habsburg and Romanov, by democrat, by
    revolutionary
At his escritoire of apple-packings, by scythe and sabre,
By Capitalismus, by oligarch and plutocrat, by Socialismus,
By Trade, by Banks and by the algebra of money,
Shaped in battle or by a kiss, shaped in the bed of your
    parents,
Shaped to inherit or to labour in disciplined factories,
Shaped to administer in La Paz or Rangoon or the
    Islands . . .
All ways of being born, Europa, the chemistry of seed and
    cell,
And our millions plundered in their lands and cities,
Bullets searching them out like inquisitive half-wits from
The mitrailleuses of Europe, shreddings of men and women.
Now as two sit in a café in a French provincial town
Served by a descendant of métissage in Guadeloupe –
She is as beautiful as the wind on the Luberon –
There is no longer in our coffee that sensation of chains
    rattled
In offshore hulks, no longer in the sifts of our sugar
A slashing of docile machetes or orations by
Abolitionists in Chambers of Commerce. She is as beautiful
As those gone down in the chronicles of Jupiter,
    metamorphosis
And elegance, as beautiful as the classics of love and
    journeys,
As beautiful as any horseman from the eastern Steppes
Who nursed an arrow to a thong and raped the Empires.
Clocks, clocks, one era replaces another, and we are dressed
In history and shaped, shaped in days, peace and war,
In the circle of blood, in the races entwined like fingers.

VII

Time's information can be heard
In that withdrawal of sound,
Respiratory suck between each tock
In the numerical flower, the clock,
Christianity's chronometer.

Beyond tea-rooms and table manners,
Mendacities and instruments,
Above a mediocre autumn we
Revolve with fragments of
Immeasurable tragedy.

On the wristwatch of christendom,
In its little warehouse of Swiss seconds
Or in the lost shadows of sundials
Are the lives of millions, stored lives
With their unmeasured stories.

VIII

Relics of the Hanseatic
Where sea is sick of the oceanic
On toy ports of the Baltic Sea
A belch of herrings, a raft of timber

The waves beyond the links and marram
Tantalize a boy who would be an explorer
Leith, Danzig, Riga and Memel,
His nationality for ever, Bordeaux and Plymouth

Courage, sea folds on itself, sea on sea,
Layer upon layer in one wet seam
Each wave of the rose-less seas
Dark fjords dreaming of tropical yellow

The boy might stitch nets in Stornoway
Or die in the Grenadines, La Rochelle,
Cadiz and Genoa, or he might command
The wooden walls of Peter the Great

Or he might live in the stews of Tortuga, or
Deliver to the slave-jetties of San Domingo,
Composing hymns as the Africans
Enter the mysteries of economics

Demerara and Coromandel, Shanghai and San Francisco,
Icebergs, fogs, and the Newfoundland Banks,
Or he might sail to Celebes and Java,
Wading ashore to wave a cutlass at the pagodas

And the seas propose their liberty
On wandering routes that lead away from
Sugar, cotton, copra and geographies
Of skin and spice, silks, silver and gold

On further seas, where no fortune is found,
No maritime shortcut or adventure, but
The poetry of man in time and lonely space,
Where no fire has been lit, no language sung

Lisbon, Venice, Bristol, Glasgow and Marseilles,
Ghost-ships at the place without a name

IX

By the banks of a Scandinavian lake
We heard harness and smalltalk
As a migrating tribe came down
To water its ponies and say goodbye.

Later a picnic happened, with white cloths,
With children and jealousies and wine,
Women holding their skirts up to their knees
Tip-toeing over these same pebbles.

Then there was Strindberg or some such,
Up to his waist in lake and shivering,
Demented with ethics, maddened
By men and women and the snow falling.

X

It was the shape of her ankle
That first suggested I desired her.
So long ago now, I cannot remember
Her place, her time, or if she spoke to me.

There was a widow at an olive press
And a girl with a sketch pad I may have married,
A waitress singing alone among her tables,
A niece who combed her old aunt's tresses.

In my long visions I have seen them again
In their wedding-clothes, under the ground,
Their white dresses spread in the flowing earth,
In the warm, geological currents.

There was a boy who bathed my brow
Before the Sultan's janissaries came over
The rubbled citadel, and the girl I met
Beneath the chandeliers in Bucharest.

In love, I've felt love like anatomy
In meditation on itself, its real
And predatory contemplations, whether
Pure and languid or disturbed by lust.

Erotic, family Europe, full of your
Philosopher-uncles of the wedding-night,
We disperse to the genders, as fires
Burn down, like wine losing its red.

XI

I rang emaciated fens.
I rang the forests. I rang the sea.
With fingernail and numerals
I dialled the animals
And they were pleased to hear from me.

I sit beside the telephone
That speaks the truth, and speak to her
As winds converse with trees and grass.
Speak to me, Europa, of dear
Munificent existences.

Say nothing of the attainable to me.
I am tired of morals and commerce.
Say nothing of history.
Tell me of your new dress
And of the scandal of happiness.

XII

We heard the ghosts of Europe
On Danubian winds
Chattering of visits to
Shadowy Prague,
Krakow, Vienna, Paris,
Rome, and talking of
Carpathian wildflowers,
The gardeners of Picardy
And geriatric pro-consuls
On their bamboo chairs
In botanic country houses,
And of the magnates of
The Côte d'Ivoire and Java,
Resplendent among their trophies.

'I shall lead you,' she said,
'Along the path of graves
From Moscow to Calais
With many detours, touching
The shores of six seas.
Those huddled in pits,
In unmarked forest graves
Or in white fields
Of multiple crucifixion,
They are our people, too.
Released from nationality
They are fraternal
In the hoax of afterlife,
Snug among the alluvials
In the republic of Europe,
As, equal at last, they drain
Into Vistula and Rhine

And a thousand rivers,
The republic of wedding-clothes
Too many citizens to be
Cause of morbidity or grief,
Their lapsed literacies
Singing in earth and water
In all our languages.
Listen. They are reality.'

XIII

Exports of British, French,
Spaniards and Portuguese,
Exports of all Europe
For wealth and colonies,
From terror and pauperdom,
Dutch, German, Jew and Pole,
Sicilian and Florentine,
Magyar, Greek and Slav,
The Scandinavians.
Here is a photograph
Of a child burned by Americans.
They plundered his skin
For he was nowhere on
Their graph of dividends.
Of all the children in the world
He is the one with no mother.
Little victim, your eyes boiled;
You became a blister.
They are no different
From the barons of Europe –
Cossacks, dragoons, a sabre
For the relish of princes.
What are we now, who have friends,
Far kin breeding this America,
Bearing our names among
The enforced Africans
Named, too, for distant kin?
Little veteran, your pain
Has innocent predecessors
In maimed childhoods on
The streets and fields of here.
Laws, music and the Renaissance,

Sea-empires of the coolies,
Accomplishments and guilt
Propose a new devotion –
To tailoring and fountain-pens,
To the export of roses,
Artichokes, poetry,
A Western innocence.
Is it to have the spirit of sheep
To close our shops to
The sale of second-hand children?

XIV

We watched them go by, in the countryside,
The cities, in remote provincial districts,
The brides and grooms of wealth and poverty.
'The dead outnumber them, the living are
Such poor creatures. In time we shall retire
To my garden, to a beloved place
That is a museum of everywhere.
There are the equatorial sculptures from
Dahomey and Benin, and there are the dollars
Minted from Incan silver, there the cross
Worn by a priest martyred by Vandals,
A stone thrown at the time of the Fronde,
Skin flayed by the Inquisition and the eyes
Of Galileo. And if you listen you can hear
The dictionaries uttered on the air,
The music of Bach and Mozart, the rhymes of Dante
In my house built of night in the mountains
And in my house built of noon on the puszta.
I mean to be benevolent and wait.
We will till the sun and shade, for purity
And light are in themselves sufficient to us.
I shall re-write the books of equity,
Engender passion, justice, love and truth
And weave a fabric of persuasive virtue.
Sleep with me. You will be my many children,
My messenger and my amanuensis.
You have nothing to lose. Give me your life
Again, and again, as I invent my cause.
I am my own mother and my daughters.
I love my people. "Our Europe is not yours."
Together we will say that again, as, once,
It was said by one of my sons to another son
In the days of souls without names smouldering
In the years of the counting of rings and teeth.'

from Elegies

In memoriam
LESLEY BALFOUR DUNN
1944–1981

Salute, o genti umane affaticate!
Tutto trapassa e nulla può morir.
Noi troppo odiammo e sofferimmo. Amate.
Il mondo è bello e santo è l'avvenir.

Carducci

Second Opinion

We went to Leeds for a second opinion.
After her name was called,
I waited among the apparently well
And those with bandaged eyes and dark spectacles.

A heavy mother shuffled with bad feet
And a stick, a pad over one eye,
Leaving her children warned in their seats.
The minutes went by like a winter.

They called me in. What moment worse
Than that young doctor trying to explain?
'It's large and growing.' 'What is?' 'Malignancy.'
'Why *there*? She's an artist!'

He shrugged and said, 'Nobody knows.'
He warned me it might spread. 'Spread?'
My body ached to suffer like her twin
And touch the cure with lips and healing sesames.

No image, no straw to support me – nothing
To hear or see. No leaves rustling in sunlight.
Only the mind sliding against events
And the antiseptic whiff of destiny.

Professional anxiety –
His hand on my shoulder
Showing me to the door, a scent of soap,
Medical fingers, and his wedding ring.

Thirteen Steps and the Thirteenth of March

She sat up on her pillows, receiving guests.
I brought them tea or sherry like a butler,
Up and down the thirteen steps from my pantry.
I was running out of vases.

More than one visitor came down, and said,
'Her room's so cheerful. She isn't afraid.'
Even the cyclamen and lilies were listening,
Their trusty tributes holding off the real.

Doorbells, shopping, laundry, post and callers,
And twenty-six steps up the stairs
From door to bed, two times thirteen's
Unlucky numeral in my high house.

And visitors, three, four, five times a day;
My wept exhaustions over plates and cups
Drained my self-pity in these days of grief
Before the grief. Flowers, and no vases left.

Tea, sherry, biscuits, cake, and whisky for the weak . . .
She fought death with an understated mischief –
'I suppose I'll have to make an effort' –
Turning down painkillers for lucidity.

Some sat downstairs with a hankie
Nursing a little cry before going up to her.
They came back with their fears of dying amended.
'Her room's so cheerful. She isn't afraid.'

Each day was duty round the clock.
Our kissing conversations kept me going,
Those times together with the phone switched off,
Remembering our lives by candlelight.

John and Stuart brought their pictures round,
A travelling exhibition. Dying,
She thumbed down some, nodded at others,
An artist and curator to the last,

Honesty at all costs. She drew up lists,
Bequests, gave things away. It tore my heart out.
Her friends assisted at this tidying
In a conspiracy of women.

At night, I lay beside her in the unique hours.
There were mysteries in candle-shadows,
Birds, aeroplanes, the rabbits of our fingers,
The lovely, erotic flame of the candlelight.

Sad? Yes. But it was beautiful also.
There was a stillness in the world. Time was out
Walking his dog by the low walls and privet.
There was anonymity in words and music.

She wanted me to wear her wedding ring.
It wouldn't fit even my little finger.
It jammed on the knuckle. I knew why.
Her fingers dwindled and her rings slipped off.

After the funeral, I had them to tea and sherry
At the Newland Park. They said it was thoughtful.
I thought it was ironic – one last time –
A mad reprisal for their loyalty.

Arrangements

'Is this the door?' This must be it. No, no.
We come across crowds and confetti, weddings
With well-wishers, relatives, whimsical bridesmaids.
Some have happened. Others are waiting their turn.
One is taking place before the Registrar.
A young groom is unsteady in his new shoes.
His bride is nervous on the edge of the future.
I walk through them with the father of my dead wife.
I redefine the meaning of 'strangers'.
Death, too, must have looked in on our wedding.
The building stinks of municipal function.
'Go through with it. You have to. It's the law.'
So I say to a clerk, 'I have come about a death.'
'In there,' she says. 'You came in by the wrong door.'

A woman with teenaged children sits at a table.
She hands to the clerk the paper her doctor gave her.
'Does that mean "heart attack"?' she asks.
How little she knows, this widow. Or any of us.
From one look she can tell I have not come
With my uncle, on the business of my aunt.
A flake of confetti falls from her fur shoulder.
There is a bond between us, a terrible bond
In the comfortless words, 'waste', 'untimely', 'tragic',
Already gossiped in the obit. conversations.
Good wishes grieve together in the space between us.
It is as if we shall be friends for ever
On the promenades of mourning and insurance,
In whatever sanatoria there are for the spirit,
Sharing the same birthday, the same predestinations.

Fictitious clinics stand by to welcome us,
Prefab'd and windswept on the edge of town
Or bijou in the antiseptic Alps,
In my case the distilled clinic of drink,
The clinic of 'sympathy' and dinners.

We enter a small office. 'What relation?' he asks.
So I tell him. Now come the details he asks for.
A tidy man, with small, hideaway handwriting,
He writes things down. He does not ask,
'Was she good?' Everyone receives this Certificate.
You do not need even to deserve it.
I want to ask why he doesn't look like a saint,
When, across his desk, through his tabulations,
His bureaucracy, his morbid particulars,
The local dead walk into genealogy.
He is no cipher of history, this one,
This recording angel in a green pullover
Administering names and dates and causes.
He has seen all the words that end in -oma.
'You give this to your undertaker.'

When we leave, this time it is by the right door,
A small door, taboo and second-rate.
It is raining. Anonymous brollies go by
In the ubiquitous urban drizzle.
Wedding parties roll up with white ribbons.
Small pools are gathering in the loving bouquets.
They must not see me. I bear a tell-tale scar.
They must not know what I am, or why I am here.
I feel myself digested in statistics of love.

Hundreds of times I must have passed this undertaker's
Sub-gothic premises with leaded windows,
By bus, on foot, by car, paying no attention.
We went past it on our first day in Hull.
Not once did I see someone leave or enter,
And here I am, closing the door behind me,
Turning the corner on a wet day in March.

France

A dozen sparrows scuttled on the frost.
We watched them play. We stood at the window,
And, if you saw us, then you saw a ghost
In duplicate. I tied her nightgown's bow.
She watched and recognized the passers-by.
Had they looked up, they'd know that she was ill –
'Please, do not draw the curtains when I die' –
From all the flowers on the windowsill.

'It's such a shame,' she said. 'Too ill, too quick.'
'I would have liked us to have gone away.'
We closed our eyes together, dreaming France,
Its meadows, rivers, woods and *jouissance*.
I counted summers, our love's arithmetic.
'Some other day, my love. Some other day.'

The Kaleidoscope

To climb these stairs again, bearing a tray,
Might be to find you pillowed with your books,
Your inventories listing gowns and frocks
As if preparing for a holiday.
Or, turning from the landing, I might find
My presence watched through your kaleidoscope,
A symmetry of husbands, each redesigned
In lovely forms of foresight, prayer and hope.
I climb these stairs a dozen times a day
And, by that open door, wait, looking in
At where you died. My hands become a tray
Offering me, my flesh, my soul, my skin.
Grief wrongs us so. I stand, and wait, and cry
For the absurd forgiveness, not knowing why.

Sandra's Mobile

A constant artist, dedicated to
Curves, shapes, the pleasant shades, the feel of colour,
She did not care what shapes, what red, what blue,
Scorning the dull to ridicule the duller
With a disinterested, loyal eye.
So Sandra brought her this and taped it up –
Three seagulls from a white and indoor sky –
A gift of old artistic comradeship.
'Blow on them, Love.' Those silent birds winged round
On thermals of my breath. On her last night,
Trying to stay awake, I saw love crowned
In tears and wooden birds and candlelight.
She did not wake again. To prove our love
Each gull, each gull, each gull, turned into dove.

Birch Room

Rotund and acrobatic tits explored
Bud-studded branches on our tallest birch tree,
A picture that came straight from her adored,
Delightfully composed chinoiserie.

She was four weeks dead before that first
Green haunting of the leaves to come, thickening
The senses with old hopes, an uncoerced
Surrender to the story of the Spring.

In summer, after dinner, we used to sit
Together in our second floor's green comfort,
Allowing nature and her modern inwit
Create a furnished dusk, a room like art.

'If only I could see our trees,' she'd say,
Bed-bound up on our third floor's wintry height.
'Change round our things, if you should choose to stay.'
I've left them as they were, in the leaf-light.

Tursac

Her pleasure whispered through a much-kissed smile.
'Oh, rock me firmly at a gentle pace!'
My love had lusty eagerness and style.
Propriety she had, preferring grace
Because she saw more virtue in its wit,
Convinced right conduct should have glamour in it
Or look good to an educated eye,
And never more than in those weeks of France
Perfected into rural elegance,
Those nights in my erotic memory.
I call that little house our *Thébaïde*
(The literary French!), and see her smile,
Then hear her in her best sardonic style:
'Write out of me, not out of what you read.'

Empty Wardrobes

I sat in a dress shop, trying to look
As dapper as a young ambassador
Or someone who'd impressed me in a book,
A literary rake or movie star.

Clothes are a way of exercising love.
False? A little. And did she like it? Yes.
Days, days, romantic as Rachmaninov,
A ploy of style, and now not comfortless.

She walked out from the changing-room in brown,
A pretty smock with its embroidered fruit;
Dress after dress, a lady-like red gown
In which she flounced, a smart career-girl's suit.

The dress she chose was green. She found it in
Our clothes-filled cabin trunk. The pot-pourri,
In muslin bags, was full of where and when.
I turn that scent like a memorial key.

But there's that day in Paris, that I regret,
When I said No, franc-less and husbandly.
She browsed through hangers in the Lafayette,
And that comes back tonight, to trouble me.

Now there is grief the couturier, and grief
The needlewoman mourning with her hands,
And grief the scattered finery of life,
The clothes she gave as keepsakes to her friends.

Creatures

A lime tree buzzed with its remembered bees.
We stood on the terrace. Fanatic prayers
Rattled with resigned displeasure. Martyrs!
'Ave!' Grasshoppers. Insect rosaries.

Nervously proud, itself, and secular,
A fox patrolled on its instinctive route
Past us and nut trees to the absolute
Wild pathless woods, a French fox, pure *renard*.

Hérisson and the encyclopaedic owl
Plotted the earth and sky of dusk. Oldest
Inhabited valley – we felt it blessed
By creatures and impacted human soul.

She said, 'The world is coming out tonight.'
Vézère's *falaises* moved grey; an ivied mist
Disguised the distance and we stood, our trust
In lizards, settling birds, the impolite

Belettes, the heavy hornets and the truths
Compiling in our senses, plain, of this life,
If inarticulate. I loved my wife.
Our two lives fluttered like two windowed moths.

She was the gentlest creature of them all.
She scattered milk-dipped bread for the lazy snakes
Asleep in the Mouliniers' bramble-brakes.
I asked her, 'Why?' 'It's only natural.'

A paradisal stasis filled the dark.
She scattered bread. 'A snake's a shy creature.'
I dip my bread in milk, and I think of her,
The châtelaine of her reasonable ark.

At the Edge of a Birchwood

Beneath my feet, bones of a little bird
Snap in a twig-flutter. A hundred wings
Adore its memory, and it is heard
In the archival choirs now where it sings.

Ewes nurse their lamb-flock on an upland field.
Late gambols in the last kick of the sun
As I scoop dirt on a hand's weight, briefly held,
A cradled cup of feathered, egg-shelled bone,

Turning the earth on it; and underground
Go song and what I feel, go common things
Into the cairn of a shoe-patted mound,
Goes half my life, go eyes, instinct and wings.

The moon rubs through the blue pallor of high east
And childlessness has no number in the May
Shadowed with birchlight on the county's crest.
This year her death-date fell on Mother's Day.

The Clear Day

Sunlight gathers in the leaves, dripping
Invisible syrups. Long afternoons
Have been reduced to this significant
Table, melodious ice cubes shaken in
A blue tumbler, lazily tipped vermouth
And a hand measuring it, a propped elbow,
A languid eye, while a reflection on
A leaf turns into everything called summer.
The heat haze ripples through the far away
Gardens of strangers, acquaintances, of those
I can put a face to. With my eyes shut,
Squeezing the soft salts of their sweat, I see
Beyond my body, nerves, cells, brain, and leisure.
Blue coastal persons walk out of the haze.
They have outflown the wind, outswum the sea.
I think, and feel, and do, but do not know
All that I am, all that I have been, once,
Or what I could be could I think of it.
These blue pedestrians bruised the edge of me
To a benign remorse, with my lessons.
With my eyes shut, I walk through a wet maze
Following a thread of sounds – birdsong in
Several cadences, children, a dog-bark,
The traffic roaring against silence as
A struck match drowns it out, simple tunes of
An amateur pianist, a vulgar shout,
A bottle tapped against a thirsty glass,
The burst of its pouring, and the slip
When the chilled glass wets a wet lower lip.
I could not guess at what the pictures are
In the eyes of a friend turned round to watch
Shrub shadows dapple a few yards of lawn

As his smoke clings to his thoughtful posture.
Tonight, I shall look out at the dark trees,
Writing this in the muddle of lost tenses
At an o'clock of flowers turned colourless.
Then, as always, the soul plays over mind
With radiantly painful speculations.
I shall sieve through our twenty years, until
I almost reach the sob in the intellect,
The truth that waits for me with its loud grief,
Sensible, commonplace, beyond understanding.

A Summer Night

Dusk softens round the leaf and cools the West.
Rhythmical fragrances, wind, grass and leaves,
Fly in and out on scented cadences.
I go into the bedroom of the world,
Discovering the long night of my life.
This telephone is electronic lies,
Ringing with calls, with farewells of the dead
Paid for on credit. Nocturnal postmen ring
My doorbell; I refuse to let them in.
My birch trees have their own two lives to lead
Without our love, although we named them us.
They play inside the aromatic wind
That is their house for ever. Outside time,
On the sensation of a memory
I walk through the dark house, remembering.
I meet the seasons on the stairs, breathing
Their pulchritudes, their four degrees of heat,
Four shades of day, shade on shade, shade on shade.
I have gone through a year, in at one end,
Out at the same way in. Same every year,
But that year was different. I counted days
As Francis counted sparrows, being kind to them.
They were not kind to me. My floating life
Borrows its fortitude from a cool silence
Composed of green, from two trees, from the tingle
That was the touch of us against the world.
It left its lived heat everywhere we'd been,
A small white cry, one last wild, stubborn rose.

Reincarnations

The kitten that befriends me at its gate
Purrs, rubs against me, until I say goodbye,
Stroking its coat, and asking 'Why? Why? Why?'
For now I know the shame of being late
Too late. She waits for me at home
Tonight, in the house-shadows. And I must mourn
Until Equator crawls to Capricorn
Or murder in the sun melts down
The Arctic and Antarctica. When bees collide
Against my study's windowpane, I let them in.
She nurtures dignity and pride;
She waters in my eye. She rustles in my study's palm;
She is the flower on the geranium.
Our little wooden train runs by itself
Along the windowsill, each puff-puff-puff
A breath of secret, sacred stuff.
I feel her goodness breathe, my Lady Christ.
Her treasured stories mourn her on their shelf,
In spirit-air, that watchful poltergeist.

Reading Pascal in the Lowlands

His aunt has gone astray in her concern
And the boy's mum leans across his wheelchair
To talk to him. She points to the river.
An aged angler and a boy they know
Cast lazily into the rippled sun.
They go there, into the dappled grass, shadows
Bickering and falling from the shaken leaves.

His father keeps apart from them, walking
On the beautiful grass that is bright green
In the sunlight of July at 7 p.m.
He sits on the bench beside me, saying
It is a lovely evening, and I rise
From my sorrows, agreeing with him.
His large hand picks tobacco from a tin;

His smile falls at my feet, on the baked earth
Shoes have shuffled over and ungrassed.
It is discourteous to ask about
Accidents, or of the sick, the unfortunate.
I do not need to, for he says 'Leukaemia'.
We look at the river, his son holding a rod,
The line going downstream in a cloud of flies.

I close my book, the *Pensées* of Pascal.
I am light with meditation, religiose
And mystic with a day of solitude.
I do not tell him of my own sorrows.
He is bored with misery and premonition.
He has seen the limits of time, asking 'Why?'
Nature is silent on that question.

A swing squeaks in the distance. Runners jog
Round the perimeter. He is indiscreet.
His son is eight years old, with months to live.
His right hand trembles on his cigarette.
He sees my book, and then he looks at me,
Knowing me for a stranger. I have said
I am sorry. What more is there to say?

He is called over to the riverbank.
I go away, leaving the Park, walking through
The Golf Course, and then a wood, climbing,
And then bracken and gorse, sheep pasturage.
From a panoptic hill I look down on
A little town, its estuary, its bridge,
Its houses, churches, its undramatic streets.

Land Love

We stood here in the coupledom of us.
I showed her this – a pool with leaping trout,
Split-second saints drawn in a rippled nimbus.

We heard the night-boys in the fir trees shout.
Dusk was an insect-hovered dark water,
The calling of lost children, stars coming out.

With all the feelings of a widower
Who does not live there now, I dream my place.
I go by the soft paths, alone with her.

Dusk is a listening, a whispered grace
Voiced on a bank, a time that is all ears
For the snapped twig, the strange wind on your face.

She waits at the door of the hemisphere
In her harvest dress, in the remote
Local August that is everywhere and here.

What rustles in the leaves, if it is not
What I asked for, an opening of doors
To a half-heard religious anecdote?

Monogamous swans on the darkened mirrors
Picture the private grace of man and wife
In its white poise, its sleepy portraitures.

Night is its Dog Star, its eyelet of grief
A high, lit echo of the starry sheaves.
A puff of hedge-dust loosens in the leaves.
Such love that lingers on the fields of life!

Home Again

Autumnal aromatics, forgotten fruits
In the bowl of this late November night,
Chastise me as I put my suitcase down.
The bowl's crystal shines and feels like frost,
And these have been the worst days of its life.
Cadaver orchard, an orphanage of pips,
Four apples sink into a pulpy rust,
And *Eat me, eat me*, says a withered pear,
Pay for your negligence and disrespect.
A scent of Burgundy – a bunch of grapes
Drinking their mortuary juice, their wrinkled skins
Dwindled and elderly black emaciations.
My six weeks gone from home portray the days
On stopped clocks and a vegetable absence.
Throw out the green loaf and bacterial cheese,
Shrunk carrots and potatoes begging for earth.
It is very lonely on the green settee,
Under the lamp, with my breath visible.
The curtains dangle in a window-sway,
In window-cold. I touch their foliage,
Their textile, sympathetic park.
I have been there in dreams, walking among
Peach-groves, and dressed in raiment of the East
In vineyards overlaid with Martagon lilies,
Arabic gardens, the south of Summerland.
Warmth is beginning and the pipes shudder.
I taste my house. Each day of its hungry gnosis,
It led a life of its own, empty of me.
The moon's oasis, the moon sipped the fruit
And the dust settled and thickened, the cold
Entered books and furniture, china and cushions.
My open suitcase mocks me from the floor.

The room is an aghast mouth. Its kiss is cold.
I think of a piano with its lid locked
And a carved, ivory silence in it.
I look.at a vase. It is too much to bear,
For it speaks of a deranged expiry,
An accusation of browned leafage.
I see the falling off of its petals
In a flashback of flowers, the white zig-zags,
A snowfall of botanic ecstasy.
A spirit shivers in the appled air,
And I know whose it is. A floral light
Bleaches my eye with angelophanous
Secrets. They are more than remembering,
Larger than sentiment. I call her name,
And it is very strange and wonderful.

The Stories

No longer are there far-flung outposts of Empire
  Where a heartsore widower could command a wall
Against the hairy raiders ignorant of commerce.
  Too much morality has interposed
Its wishy-washy journalism and hope. Who am I
  To weep for Salvador or Kampuchea
When I am made the acolyte of my own shadow?
  Grief has its own romance, its comedy,
Its preposterous and selfish gestures. Men and women,
  Who, one day, will feel as I do now, I
Empty my heart, my head, dreaming again of days
  Gone by in another life. I could sail North
To Spitzbergen, to the iced-over mountainous islands
  Outlined on charts of the glacial deltas,
Or south to the rainforests, or to the blank of sands
  Drifting like the heartlessness of time.
Where is the frontier I could serve with a paid sword
  Dutiful to an imperial ass who lavishes
His days on orthodox, abstruse theology
  And his exchequer on a paradise
To please the gluttony of his heretical consort?
  At my age, I could die splendidly on
A staircase, unarmed, banished, but soldierly, before
  The spears and sabres of the wicked host
That trumped my preparations and stole the city
  In the name of their Prophet. I could have died
On the trails of exploration, under the sun or the arrows.
  And what religion is left now, to serve
With local Caledonian sainthood, stern, but kind,
  Baptizing the baby Africans, and plodding
To a discovery of God and waterfalls?
  Nor are there any longer those unvisited isles

Where a beachcomber might scrounge a boozy salvation.
    To meditate in a tropical hovel –
Palm leaves, creeper, coconut shells, jettisoned containers –
    On wheretofores, buts, ifs and perhapses,
Over that anguished prose of what we think we deserve,
    Or don't deserve, but live with, either way,
Would be a perfect if anti-social philosophizing,
    Doubtless illogical, or arrogant,
Or windily puffed-up to heights of self-deception.
    Interior ethics, like oncogenic catastrophes,
Happen anywhere, the melanomas of the sun
    Or the occult surprises of contemplation.
Why grieve like this? I loathe my bitter, scorning wit,
    This raffish sorrow artificed by stories.
I can see myself in a jungle-drunk's smeared linen suit
    Under the fan in a lost trading post,
Most Maugham-ish in my matutinal repartee
    At my breakfast of mango and whisky
As the steamer arrives, delicate with white nuns
    And crates of Haig and quinine, the new clerk
Already mothered on the rack of a malarial fever.
    There are a thousand plots in the narrative
In which grief is the hero. In these frequent stories
    There is always somewhere to go to, outbacks,
Exiles, White Men's Graves where piratical gun-runners
    Mix with evangelists, where wilderness
Brings out the worst of men as well as charity,
    Where sacrifice embroiders every tale
And the devoted nun weeps in the shot-up pagoda
    As a Chicagoan's lung-blood soaks her arms.
Breast-plated with Gustavus Adolphus and Dalgetty,
    I could have lost myself in Baltic syntax.
Foot-slogging the Sahara with kepi, pack and gun,
    I could have made the beautiful gesture,
The joke of spitting in Death's broad, fictitious grin.

[256]

It is no longer the world of the stories.
Opportunities for a ludicrous public service,
   For the lunacy of last-ditch duty
To Monarch, regiment or John Company,
   Are stoic options stored in Yesterday.
Why be discreet? A broken heart is what I have –
   A pin to burst the bubble of shy poetry,
Mnemosyne revealed as what, in life, she stands for.
   I shall observe the moods of the great sky,
The flight of herons, the coming into leaf of birches
   And the religious glow on ancient waves
Breaking against *Candida casa* of the cliffs.
   If you should see me, or one of my kind,
Looking out to the far ocean from a lonely headland,
   Or walking by the hedgerows, then turn away.
Walk on by, and leave us there to remember and dream
   Our speculative visions of the past
Narrated through the legendary, retrospective fictions,
   Tales of anachronism. Such days they were!
Not even that sweet light garnishing Sisyphean innocence
   Redeems me, dedicated to the one
Pure elegy, looking as if I like the way I am.
   I do not; for I would rather that I could die
In the act of giving, and prove the truth of us
   Particular, eternal, by doing so
Be moral at the moment of the good death, showing
   An intimate salvation beyond the wish
Merely to die, but to be, for once, commendable.

Anniversaries

Day by nomadic day
Our anniversaries go by,
Dates anchored in an inner sky,
To utmost ground, interior clay.
    It was September blue
When I walked with you first, my love,
In Roukenglen and Kelvingrove,
Inchinnan's beech-wood avenue.
    That day will still exist
Long after I have joined you where
Rings radiate the dusty air
And bangles bind each powdered wrist.
    Here comes that day again.
What shall I do? Instruct me, dear,
Longanimous encourager,
Sweet Soul in the athletic rain
    And wife now to the weather.

        Glaswegian starlings fly
In their black cape, a fluttered noise,
Ornithological hurrahs
From spires in the November sky.
        The Candleriggs is husks
And cabbage leaves, a citric scent,
A vegetable sentiment,
Closed apple-depots in the dusk's
        Indigenous metaphor –
Arcadian orchards of the lost
On this Bohemian sea-coast
And exits, pursued by a bear.
        I passed our wedding day
Drunk on the salad street, a null
White-out of loss and alcohol;
Your ring, our anniversary,
        And starlings in my soul.

        A liquid light sips dew
From how it is as blossoms foam
With May's arboreal aplomb
Against a reminiscent blue.
        Day, number, memory,
Kissed hours when day's door hangs ajar
And light crawls on the calendar,
Each routine anniversary
        At night, and noon, and dawn,
Are times I meet you, when souls rinse
Together in their moist reunions.
Iambic, feathery Anon
        Opens anthologies,
Born and reborn, as days go by
In anniversaries of sky
When oceans cradle little seas
        That water in the eye.

My diaries are days,
Flesh days and real. The calendar
Recurs to tell us who we are,
Or were, to praise or to dispraise.
    Here is a day come round
Again. This window's a wet stone
I can't see through. Daylight and sun,
Reflectionless, a glassy ground,
    It slides on vitreous space.
I shiver in the memory
And sculpt my foolish poetry
From thwarted life and snapped increase.
    Cancer's no metaphor.
Bright rain-glass on the window's birch
This supernatural day of March,
Dwindled, come dusk, to one bright star,
    Cold and compassionate.

Hush

Shh. Sizzle of days, weeks, months, years . . .
How much of us has gone, rising and crying.
My skin seeps its pond of dew.

Air sips and licks as I walk out today
In the transparent jaw of the weather
When the first leaves are greening.

Behind me I can hear
A click of fantasy heels,
But there is no one there.

She is with me, as I call to see
A sick friend whose skin is drying
On the bones of her spirit.

I stand on the sad threshold with my flowers.
How old this is, and how the heart beats faster
As I wait at the bell like a mourning wooer,

As the dog barks, as I give my flowers
And a secret wind blows in from eternal woods,
As my flowers sigh, asking for water.

Leaving Dundee

A small blue window opens in the sky
As thunder rumbles somewhere over Fife.
Eight months of up-and-down – goodbye, goodbye –
Since I sat listening to the wild geese cry
Fanatic flightpaths up autumnal Tay,
Instinctive, mad for home – make way! make way!
Communal feathered scissors, cutting through
The grievous artifice that was my life,
I was alert again, and listening to
That wavering, invisible V-dart
Between two bridges. Now, in a moistened puff,
Flags hang on the château-stacked gables of
A 1980s expense account hotel,
A lost French fantasy, baronial.
From here, through trees, its Frenchness hurts my heart.
It slips into a library of times.
Like an eye on a watch, it looks at me.
And I am going home on Saturday
To my house, to sit at my desk of rhymes
Among familiar things of love, that love me.
Down there, over the green and the railway yards,
Across the broad, rain-misted, subtle Tay,
The road home trickles to a house, a door.
She spoke of what I might do 'afterwards'.
'Go, somewhere else.' I went north to Dundee.
Tomorrow I won't live here any more,
Nor leave alone. *My love, say you'll come with me.*